Work-Based Research in the Early Years

Education at SAGE

SAGE is a leading international publisher of journals, books, and electronic media for academic, educational, and professional markets.

Our education publishing includes:

- accessible and comprehensive texts for aspiring education professionals and practitioners looking to further their careers through continuing professional development

- inspirational advice and guidance for the classroom

- authoritative state of the art reference from the leading authors in the field

Find out more at: **www.sagepub.co.uk/education**

Work-Based Research in the Early Years

Sue Callan and Michael Reed

SAGE

Los Angeles | London | New Delhi
Singapore | Washington DC

Editorial arrangement and introduction © Sue Callan and
Michael Reed 2011

Chapter 1 © Sue Callan, Linda Picken and Sue Foster 2011
Chapter 2 © Carla Solvason 2011
Chapter 3 © Victoria Cooper and Carole Ellis 2011
Chapter 4 © Jude Simms and Sue Callan 2011
Chapter 5 © Tracy Davies, Carole Ellis and Alison Jackson 2011
Chapter 6 © Sharon Smith, Michael Reed and Sue Callan 2011
Chapter 7 © Sue Callan and Linda Tyler 2011
Chapter 8 © Joy Cullen, Helen Hedges and Jane Bone 2011

First published 2011

SAGE Publications Ltd
1 Oliver's Yard
55 City Road
London EC1Y 1SP

SAGE Publications Inc.
2455 Teller Road
Thousand Oaks, California 91320

SAGE Publications India Pvt Ltd
B 1/I 1 Mohan Cooperative Industrial Area
Mathura Road
New Delhi 110 044

SAGE Publications Asia-Pacific Pte Ltd
33 Pekin Street #02-01
Far East Square
Singapore 048763

Library of Congress Control Number: 2010942722

British Library Cataloguing in Publication data

A catalogue record for this book is available from the British Library

ISBN 978-0-85702-174-8
ISBN 978-0-85702-175-5 (pbk)

Typeset by C&M Digitals (P) Ltd, Chennai, India
Printed in India at Replika Press Pvt Ltd
Printed on paper from sustainable resources

Contents

List of figures and tables

Figures

Table

List of abbreviations

AERA   American Educational Research Association

BERA   British Educational Research Association

CCSK   Common Core of Skills and Knowledge

CPD   continuing professional development

CWDC Children's Workforce Development Council

DCSF   Department for Children, Schools and Families

DfEE   Department for Education and Employment

DfES   Department for Education and Skills

ECAP   Early Childhood and Parenting Collaborative

ECRP   *Early Childhood Research and Practice*

EYFS   Early Years Foundation Stage

EYP   Early Years Professional

FDA   Foundation Degree Award

ICT   information and communications technology

SAED   social and emotional development

SEF   self-evaluation form

SERA   Scottish Educational Research Association

About the editors and contributors

Editors

Sue Callan is an Associate Lecturer with the Open University, teaching on both the Primary Teaching and Learning and Early Years Foundation Degrees. She is an experienced author and is currently involved with a small-scale research project within the Open University. Sue has been involved with Foundation Degrees in Early Years since 2003 and has worked in further and higher education since 1990, specialising in community-based pre-school practice and working with mature students in both personal tutoring and mentoring roles. She is a contributor to *Mentoring in the Early Years* and co-editor of *Managing Early Years Settings*, both published by Sage.

Michael Reed works for part of his time as a Senior Lecturer at the Centre for Early Childhood, within the Institute of Education at the University of Worcester. He teaches on undergraduate and postgraduate courses and shares a coordinating role for a large Foundation Degree programme in early years, taught in partner colleges and in children's centres within the community. He was also part of the writing and development team for the Early Years Foundation Degree at the Open University. He co-edited *Reflective Practice in the Early Years* and most recently *Implementing Quality Improvement and Change in the Early Years*, both published by Sage.

Contributors

Jane Bone researches and lectures in the area of Early Childhood Education and after many years in New Zealand she is now at

Monash University, Australia. Her expertise is in holistic approaches to pedagogy and learning and she has particular research interests in the area of spirituality, values, beliefs and ethics. Involvement in these sensitive areas of research contributes to wider understandings about the significance of early childhood education in terms of diversity, indigenous knowledge, well-being and social justice. Her work is internationally recognised and she is currently a Visiting Scholar at University College Oslo, Norway.

Victoria Cooper is a member of the academic module team for Childhood, Development and Learning at the Open University. She teaches across a range of undergraduate and postgraduate early years educational research, health and social care programmes. She is post-graduate module chair of Children and Young People's Worlds: Developing Frameworks for Integrated Practice and Understanding Children's Development and Learning. Her background is as an early years teacher, research psychologist and a lecturer in further and higher education. Her research interests include children's identity, mental health and the education of young people.

Joy Cullen was formerly Professor of Early Years Education at Massey University, Palmerston North, New Zealand. She has worked in early childhood teacher education since 1982, in Australia and New Zealand, providing academic leadership for programmes from certificate to doc-toral level. Her research in early years education encompasses national survey research to research support for teacher research in New Zealand's early childhood Centre of Innovation programme. She chaired the Ethics Committee, College of Education, Massey University. She is joint editor of *Early Childhood Education: Society and Culture*. Joy now lives in Australia where she continues to publish in early years education.

Tracy Davies has worked with children for 18 years, starting out as a helper at a toddler group, then leading the group before becoming a childminder. Similarly, she began helping in school as a parent reader and soon became involved as a classroom assistant before working as a nursery nurse in day care – all the while continuing in vocational professional development. Tracy returned to a small pri-mary school as an Special Educational Needs teaching assistant and has since completed a BA (Hons) in Integrated Early Childhood Studies. She continues to work in school where she has responsibility for implementing ICT in Key Stages 1 and 2.

Carole Ellis is a family support worker based in a children's centre in South Herefordshire. In her role as part of a multi-professional team supporting community development and family engagement with local services, Carole uses a play-based approach to supporting children and their families. She is an experienced practitioner with a background as a nursery nurse and senior teaching assistant, supporting children through play for more than 20 years. Carole has contributed to developing local practice in working with fathers groups, based on her Foundation Degree research project.

Sue Foster 'fell' into childcare nearly 30 years ago while working in the business sector and looking for a suitable nursery for her son. She began as a childminder in partnership with a colleague and soon set up her own very small private nursery in Worcestershire, which unusually has all age groups mixed together. She first qualified with an NNEB but, through progressive continuing professional development, has recently achieved an Honours degree in Early Childhood and holds Early Years Practitioner Status. Her nursery now provides care and learning for 50 children.

Helen Hedges is a Senior Lecturer in early years curriculum at the Faculty of Education, University of Auckland, New Zealand. Her research programme investigates children's and teachers' knowledge, interests and ongoing learning and enquiry, and ways these coalesce to co-construct interests-based curriculum in early years settings. She co-edited *Theorising Early Childhood Practice: Emerging Dialogues* in which she co-authored a chapter on practitioner research. She has also published on ethical research with child participants and designing research to connect research, practice and professional learning for teachers.

Alison Jackson is an early years practitioner with over 20 years' experience working with children under eight in a range of settings. She has been a nursery supervisor and is an accredited childminder with Early Years Professional status. Her experience has included acting as chair of a pre-school management committee and chair of her county Childminding Association. She is a member of her local Early Years and Extended Services Forum and an early years representative to the county Schools Forum. Alison is completing a BA (Hons) in Integrated Early Childhood Studies and has recently gained Early Years Professional Status. She has contributed to publications on reflective practice for Sage.

Liz Olliver is a Deputy Manager of a 100-place children's nursery school in South Herefordshire. She has 15 years' experience practising in the field of early years in a variety of roles including nanny, au pair in America, teaching assistant in a primary school and several positions in under-eight provisions across the country. She has recently gained her

Early Years Professional Status and is currently completing her BA (Hons) in Integrated Childhood Studies at the University of Worcester.

Linda Picken has worked with babies, young children and their families in various contexts for over 20 years. Linda is currently working as an Infant Toddler Room Supervisor – part of a children's centre in Herefordshire. Both the nursery and the centre work with the values and vision encapsulated within the Reggio Emilia approach. Linda holds a BA (Hons) Degree in Early Childhood Studies and has gained Early Years Professional Status (EYPS) from the University of Worcester.

Jude Simms is an Early Years Professional in England, responsible for a split-site community-run setting. In addition to a Fine Arts degree, she has a BA (Hons) in Early Childhood and is currently studying for a Master's degree at the University of Worcester. Jude is a Community Governor in a First School and works alongside a Health Visitor in a local group for new parents and their babies

Sharon Smith is a Lecturer at South Worcestershire College and for the University of Worcester. She has been involved in the development and delivery of Foundation Degrees (FdA's) and has a passion for Lifelong Learning. Within her expertise she has been instrumental in using online tools to deliver FdAs and has been involved in a range of JISC projects. Sharon is committed to the ongoing development of FdAs and is an external Examiner for two courses at this level at Roehampton University. Her Master's dissertation reflected on the delivery of higher education in further education institutions. As a Foundation Governor in a local school she believes that community cohesion is important for the development of children's education as well as their social and spiritual development.

Carla Solvason is a Senior Lecturer in the Centre for Early Childhood within the Institute of Education at the University of Worcester. Part of her role involves working closely with the eight partner colleges that deliver the university's Foundation Degree in Early Years. She teaches on the BA, FdA, PGCE and Masters programmes and is a research degree supervisor. Prior to lecturing Carla worked as a researcher, a consultant for schools looking to create communication-rich environments and a primary school teacher. Carla has published work relating to school culture and educational equality and social justice.

Linda Tyler is a Senior Lecturer and Course Leader for the Integrated Early Childhood Studies degree within the Institute of Education at the University of Worcester. Previously, she has worked as a teacher and coordinator for ICT, Literacy and Science in a Becta award-winning school. She has designed and delivered ICT training for a local authority and developed several ICTogether groups to enhance ICT skills working with parents and children. She is researching the effects of podcasting on children's communication skills in order to develop a Teacher Training package for students. She has published works online about the use of avatars as a medium for improving literacy – a feature of her PhD interest.

Acknowledgements

The editors would like to acknowledge the work of all the contributors to this text and particularly the featured practitioners who have provided their experience of work-based research in order to illustrate our discussion. This must also include Sarah Rosser and Melanie Pilcher for help and feedback during the development of the manuscript and to Peter Butler for preparation of the final text. Thanks also to Amy Jarrold, Alex Molineux and Jude Bowen at Sage Publications for help, patience and enthusiasm throughout the project and for facilitating our shared work with colleagues in New Zealand. In every respect this book is a genuine collaborative effort – with all the fun and fear that such an approach entails.

This book is written for all colleagues within the early years sector and for the children and families with whom they work.

Sue Callan dedicates this book to Peter who makes everything possible and in memory of Mum and Dad – Louie and Andy Yule. All authors dedicate the text to: Michael, Jonathan, Issac, James, Arran, Sammy-Lee, Melina, Tess, Joshua, Jacob, Alex, Ellen, Euan, Emma, Dominic, Jess, Jaz, Sophie, Olivia, Jamie, Jack, Imogen, Rebecca, Chris. And parents and children everywhere.

This book offers an excellent collection of chapters which encourage early years practitioners to examine their practice in the light of research concepts and gain an understanding of the processes of preparing for, doing and learning from research. The book bridges practice and research, by articulating and exemplifying them as rigorous, thorough and ethical encounters and illustrates that work-based research is as meaningful and important as academic research. Highly recommended for everyone who thinks to conduct research in their own work place.

Theodora Papatheodorou, Anglia Ruskin University

This informative and stimulating book on the realities of professional enquiry in early years' settings will provide an invaluable support as practitioners respond to the demand to evidence their practice rigorously and systematically. The authors have succeeded in making practitioner research interesting, accessible, do-able and directly relevant to those concerned with developing the quality of police and practice in the field.

Professor Christine Pascal, Director of the Centre for Research in Early Childhood

Introduction: Work-based research in the early years – positioning yourself as a researcher

Michael Reed and Sue Callan

This book seeks to explain in practical terms the *process* that practitioners experience as they engage in 'research' – a word used interchangeably in the book alongside 'enquiry', 'evaluation' or 'investigations'. We also add 'practice-based' or 'work-based' to give emphasis to the way it is rooted in early years settings. The book has a distinct focus on process which we see as an extension of 'intuitive' and reflective practice which is at the heart of continued professional development. This is not (nor does it wish to be) a book that tells you 'how to write a dissertation'. Indeed, there are many such books available and we are not in any way setting out to denigrate or move aside from such important texts. In fact we have used some in our construction of the book. Instead, we seek to illustrate how daily experience of working with children and families drives forward ways to engage in small-scale enquiry in early years settings. We argue that underpinning this drive is an essential component of any research – *purpose*: an aspect which is considered in more detail by Carla Solvason in her chapter. The book is drawn from the shared reflections of established academic authors as well as the experiences of practitioners who have engaged in practice-based research during their professional development. Together, they provide a repertoire of views that illustrate ways to investigate and improve the quality of early years provision. We hope the book will inspire you to engage in the kind of critical reflective practice that characterises research-engaged teams (Hedges and Cullen, 2005).

Our starting point is the view that any critical reflective evaluation of practice is an integrated part of the Every Child Matters agenda (DfES, 2004). This agenda has permeated each of the nations of the UK in terms of developing early years curriculum frameworks. There is now a consensus in the UK about the value of a play-based curriculum and the need for continuing professional development, supporting parents, and protecting and enhancing the welfare of children. It is seen as essential that professionals work together to provide 'joined up' working and consider the 'whole child' within the family and the curriculum. These are important 'contributing factors' which are prompting us to investigate the way we do things in practice. Some of these are illustrated in Figure 1.

The diagram illustrates the pace, direction and sheer volume of change that some might see as representing nothing more than a top-down model of regulatory intrusion. It is when we respond to these initiatives that we understand the *purpose* for practice-based research. This allows us to accept aspects that improve practice and challenge those we think do not. This view is supported by Wenger (2010) who suggests that although regulations are influential and inform practice, they do not produce practice. He suggests that policies and regulation can also inhibit practitioners from using their own knowledge, experience and creativity to help improve practice and move forward. This is important because it tells us about the inherent value of practice-based enquiry – the way it can free practitioners from an obsession with reviewing what they are told to review and move on to what is important to them: their settings and the children in their care. This is not to suggest we throw away all of the positive aspects of Every Child Matters (DfES, 2004), it is more to do with carefully selecting and examining what is important to local settings, offering an alternative to the regulatory and curriculum demands and seeing practice-based investigation as a 'bottom-up' process rather than always 'top down'. To do this practitioners require the tools and training to aid the process, foremost of which is the knowledge, confidence and ability to investigate practice. We hope this book will play some small part in developing these skills. Having said this, we are also realistic and it is impossible to ignore the fact that practitioners are busy and committed people. They are responding to a range of initiatives while still supporting families and improving quality. Time to engage in research is precious,

Practice-based investigation is increasingly part of practice.

The diagram illustrates factors which have driven forward change. It also illustrates the range of interrelated, but sometimes competing demands that require evaluation of practice.

Regulatory or inspection frameworks. These consider if practice is developing. They require a review of practice and self-evaluation. **Integrated/partnership working is evaluated.**

National Curriculum frameworks protect the welfare of children and enhance learning. They require practice and policies to be reviewed and evaluated.

Policies and practices within settings. They are part of practice and for practice. They help to forge **communities of practice** between people at local level. They are often the subject of review and evaluation.

There are **guidance and coordinated strategies** which ask practitioners to work together in order to protect vulnerable children, for example common assessment frameworks. Settings are often asked to review their practice and the efficiency of these strategies.

Workforce development organisations consider professional expectations placed upon practitioners. These include the ability to reflect and investigate and lead practice.

Quality improvement frameworks look at many aspects of practice, for example **integrated working**, and asks practitioners to investigate practice. The voluntary **sector is more fully integrated into any review of practice.**

National policies, plans and directives – policies are enacted at local level and **inform planning** within early years settings. Policies are the subject of review.

Advice, training and qualifications – early childhood training programmes at colleges and universities all promote practice-based investigation as a means to learn and engage in leading practice.

Parents are encouraged to participate and play an active part in developing practice. Practitioners often evaluate parent partnership initiatives.

Diagram adapted with permission from Reed and Canning (2011).

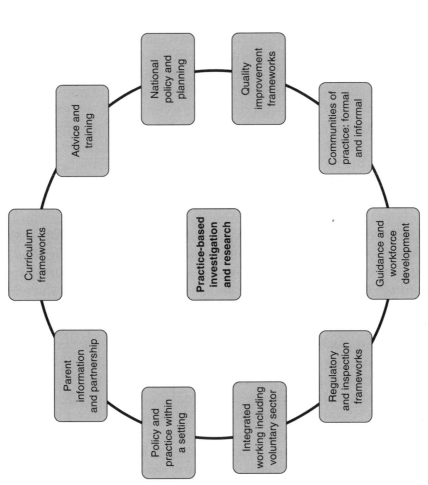

Figure 1 Representing practice-based investigation and research

which is why 'insider-focused' research – looking at practice while engaged in practice – is so important. Inevitably this stance has coincided with a wider debate about the role and responsibilities of those involved in working with children and their families and the very nature of what should constitute a competent, adaptive, reflective practitioner. It is in this context that we see the investigation of *practice* and *research* as being of such importance. We argue that the terms are not mutually exclusive and are often mutually responsive. They represent ways that practitioners engage in and 'position' themselves. This may be as an 'insider' who is an integral part of an early years setting, holding information and searching for information based upon their day-to-day practice, or as an 'outsider' who engages in research in one or more settings, exploring specific aspects of the practice of others. Costley et al. (2010) give an informed view of such 'positioning' which includes the influence of universities and colleges on the process, the importance of maintaining an ethical stance as an 'insider-researcher' and the responsibility this places on a practitioner in terms of the roles and responsibilities in the workplace. Goodfellow (2007) also explores how practitioners engage in research and concludes that professional enquiry sits well with early childhood professionals because they value reflection and are always concerned with refining their approaches to working with children. She argues that this can be inhibited by issues surrounding time, a lack of appreciation of undertaking such research activity and the need for leadership in the process. There are also those who have explored the advantages and disadvantages of being an 'insider' or an 'outsider' and the work of Wadsworth (1997) offers a summary of the tensions and dilemmas facing the insider/outsider researcher.

It is suggested that insiders have an in-depth knowledge of their world but may be too 'caught up' in day-to-day practice and need to distance themselves from what goes on. Outsiders can, however, have an advantage: they can ask questions, sometimes difficult questions that have not previously been asked and which shed light on practice. They can also see things from a distance and as a consequence may propose innovative solutions. Nevertheless, they can sometimes (to an insider) state the obvious in which case their voice might not be easily heard.

We must also understand the underlying perceptions of what is meant by 'research'. It is all too easy to see this as a research report or

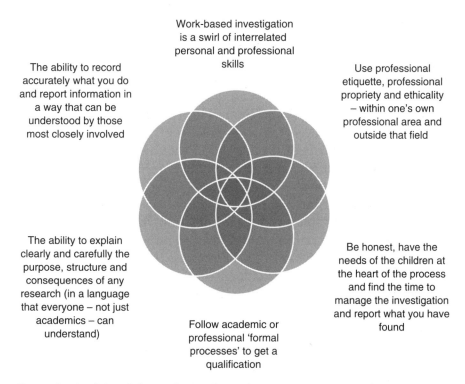

The ability to record accurately what you do and report information in a way that can be understood by those most closely involved

Work-based investigation is a swirl of interrelated personal and professional skills

Use professional etiquette, professional propriety and ethicality – within one's own professional area and outside that field

The ability to explain clearly and carefully the purpose, structure and consequences of any research (in a language that everyone – not just academics – can understand)

Follow academic or professional 'formal processes' to get a qualification

Be honest, have the needs of the children at the heart of the process and find the time to manage the investigation and report what you have found

Figure 2 Qualities of the professional practitioner

dissertation (for examination at a college or university), in which case the whole process can become quite formal. This is because in academic contexts students are often advised that there is usually a standard way of engaging in an investigation and reporting what was found leading to a conclusion or tentative conclusion – with perhaps recommendations for action or change. On the other hand, an investigation may be part of and emerge from working practice. It may share some of the attributes of a formal report but have more to do with day-to-day quality improvement with the purpose of making current practice more visible/viable or suggesting how existing practice might be improved. In work-based research, the 'audience' are those most closely involved and this requires quite intense reflection on practice. Work-based investigation may be short term, it may require fairly immediate action and it may look forward as well as back. Both approaches, be they 'formal' or 'informal', require more than a system of enquiry or stages of investigation and rely upon a multiplicity of interrelated skills and abilities that can be seen in Figure 2.

These 'abilities' require professional skills, a pronounced ethical stance, accuracy, personal qualities, and good communication and negotiating skills. Similarly, professional and personal responses to the question 'Why am I doing this?' are also required. The answer might cover a range of responses: to get a qualification or improve practice or inform parents. It could be to do with wanting to find out more in order to lead practice or change practice. It might be because an inspection is imminent or it could be to gain an award. It might be to aid professional development. It could be to improve work with a voluntary group or another discipline or setting. There will always be a multiplicity of reasons for engaging in an investigation. The only certainty is that engaging in an investigation will change how you view the world and it will no doubt have an impact on practice – and in some cases, probably both. This is because investigation is inextricably linked to the process of change. It provides the researcher with a critically reflective view about what goes on and makes the ordinary quite special (Le Gallais, 2004). If there is a subtext for the whole book, this is it: we see work-based investigation as just as meaningful and as representative of practitioner experience as the academic or large-scale projects which inform national context in the UK. Moreover, the two are not mutually exclusive as the investigative experience can inform ways in which a setting can interpret and understand national policies. The relationship between the two takes us back to the start of this introduction: work-based investigation supports the premise of Every Child Matters (DfES, 2004), is a foundation for improving children's welfare and has immediacy in enhancing their experiences in settings on a day-to-day basis.

Positioning ourselves

Any book with a focus on work-based investigation, evaluation or enquiry has to take into account the way the professional world of early childhood has changed and is changing. Perhaps the only certainty in terms of early childhood education is the certainty that we shall need to adapt and respond to change (Reed and Sansoyer, 2011) – change which has led to a range of qualifications, policies and directives throughout the UK. These place high levels of expectation upon practitioners which are well intentioned but sometimes give a 'technocratic' view of early years practice. Targets are set, professional expectations provided from the top down and regulation is seen as a mark of quality. We prefer to think more about the qualities and 'professional dispositions' that can be seen in practice (Rike and Sharp, 2008). We see practitioners who are engaged in research already demonstrating a personal interrelationship with the setting and fulfilling a desire to improve quality in parallel to and building upon their existing roles, responsibilities and relationships with children and families. It is clear these provide a framework for engaging in what we call research and, as such, are represented in the practitioner investigations in all subsequent chapters. For example, look at some of the skills and dispositions that a practitioner already holds.

- providing a warm, caring and purposeful way of effectively communicating with others, with children, young people and families – this is an essential part of research;

- acting ethically and professionally in their work with children and families – such standards are part and parcel of research;

- looking through different landscapes of professional practice and the eyes of different professional groups – this is something practitioners are encouraged to do by directives and policies surrounding early years practice – it is also an expectation placed upon researchers;

- showing an ability to be curious about a child's development, the way children are taught and how they learn as well as what they learn – this disposition is expected of a practitioner and is an important asset for any researcher;

- being an advocate for the child and demonstrating practice which safeguards the welfare of the child – again, an essential part of research practice;

- leading practice, sharing expertise, acting as a critical friend to others and responding positively to change – this is certainly expected of practitioners and is an asset to any researcher;

- understanding and applying aspects of diversity and inclusion to promote the welfare of children – an aspect of practice that should be modelled by a sensitive, responsive researcher;

- improving quality and providing access to that quality for disadvantaged groups – something that adds real and substantive purpose to any research;

- understanding the importance of developing a positive learning environment and being careful and sensitive to the needs of children when exploring the environment – again, an essential component for any research;

- regarding continuing professional development (CPD) as an important aspect of professional practice – researchers attempt to develop this perspective from 'doing research' at a personal and professional level;

- reflecting on practice and challenging practice while having a responsibility to parents, other practitioners and children – an inherent positive disposition that all researchers strive to develop.

All of these are laudable aspects of early years professionalism. They tell us that practitioners *are* 'researchers'. They do have the skills, the attitude and the ability to engage in enquiry. The danger is that just articulating these descriptors results in yet another set of competencies and professional objectives – indeed, a set of 'requirements' that can somehow be taught. We suggest they are instead seen as professional attributes which are already in place and can be refined and developed by values, beliefs, personal heritage and professional skills. Inevitably, this means a degree of reflection from practitioners, something that we argue should be part of work-based evaluation and investigation which may well cause a review of professional and personal roles and responsibilities. Moss (2010) sees such a review as a necessity and suggests we need to carefully reconsider in order to redefine roles. He sees this as a political and ethical choice that needs to start with critical questions about how the work of an early years practitioner is understood and what values are considered important. There is also the work of Osgood (2009) who considers the opportunities available for alternative constructions of professionalism to take shape from within communities of early years practice. There are also those who offer critical perspectives on the way a drive towards qualifications are inhibiting professionalism (Lloyd and Hallet, 2010a). It is clear that the debate is unlikely to rest and there is a continuing interest in this facet of education (Osgood, 2006, 2010; Lloyd and Hallet, 2010b). Added to this is the wider issue of pay, service conditions and status in the workforce (Cooke and Lawton, 2008). Similarly, there are continued tensions in professional hierarchies within early childhood qualifications. It is therefore important when constructing our own 'position' that we recognise the powerful responses that are emerging about the way practitioners are developing their practice. We would also argue that exploring the curriculum in itself is not enough to make judgements about the way in which approaches to children's care and education are implemented. Lubek (1995) argued that wider considerations such as the national economic agenda and ideological perspectives need to be taken into account when analysing similarities and differences. New (2008) examines these considerations and suggests we need to debate the relative importance of national goals versus cultural values in determining priorities for young children. In particular, we should consider the view that practitioners are the informants of social policy. This resonates with our view that 'collaborative enquiry' is a means to elicit views on what is happening and what works, and this requires a reflexive stance when considering individual and collective perspectives, a stance that is usefully explained by Finlay and Gough who suggest:

> Reflexive means to 'bend back on oneself'. In research terms this can be translated as thoughtful, self-aware analysis of the inter-subjective dynamics between researcher and the researched. Reflexivity requires critical self-reflection of the ways in which researchers' social background, assumptions, positioning behaviour impact upon the research process. (2003: 9)

Therefore in this book when we offer a view on what may constitute effective research and an examination of the processes involved, we are not constructing truths, but only interpretations that can be probed and reconstructed (Hertz, 1997). Our position is clear: we argue there is a generation of practitioners who have known little in their professional lives but change. They are, however, developing their own views and their voices are starting to be heard (Callan, 2007; Smith, 2008). It is clear that contemporary practice requires professional attributes and qualities which cross service boundaries, in essence encompassing the view that 'children do not distinguish their needs based on which agencies run which services – neither should we' (DfES, 2004: 20). This requires the ability to think critically in applying policy while trying to keep the child and the family at the centre. It requires knowledge and understanding of structural aspects and a consideration of values and beliefs at a personal level, a process that we see as being aided by engaging in study that embeds reflective practice into work-based training (Reed, 2011; Callan et al., 2010; Canning and Callan, 2010; Dochy et al., 2011), and which Appleby (2010) sees as developing personal confidence and motivation to construct an interpretation of what it means for individuals to work in a particular context. This we see as important to enable practitioners to determine where they 'fit' in terms of contributing to early years change and development. Claxton (2003) views this process as a never-ending 'learning journey' involving personal and professional qualities that merge as we develop a personal sense of responsibility and share our knowledge – in effect forging a 'community or landscape of practice' (Wenger, 1998; Wenger et al., 2002). To do this requires a change in learning culture from first a culture of knowledge transfer that involves being taught what to do as well as why it is done, second a culture of dialogue, interaction and challenge, and third a culture of heutagogy which places specific emphasis on learning how to learn and encourages learner self-direction, in effect the ability to engage in purposeful, meaningful, practice-based evaluation.

How is this illustrated in the book?

Most chapters draw upon the views of established writers in the field. Others are the result of a partnership between established authors and experienced practitioners who have conducted research and evaluated practice as part of the requirement for academic qualification. The chapters are designed to:

- clarify thinking and ideas about the nature of work-based investigations, in particular where and how you 'position yourself';

- articulate for practitioners how their 'intuitive' self is represented in academic constructs such as 'methodology';

- support the small, informal processes apparent in day-to-day practice that may not require an academic, research report, but could benefit from a sensitivity to ethical leadership and management issues;

- support the emerging and continued reflection of practitioners in the sector, in particular as they seek to respond to proposed change or review of curriculum frameworks;

- introduce further reading and direct the reader towards books and materials that allow them to explore 'reflective practice, work-based enquiry and quality improvement;

- offer a practical explanation of research for undergraduate students and underline the need for purpose in what they do.

Our overview of chapters is a guide to what is *in* the book, not an indication of how to *use* the book. This is an important distinction because we do not wish to present a 'linear' view of the research process. Instead, we see the book as a resource to inform and support practitioner investigations. Indeed, throughout the text, all colleagues emphasise that work-based investigation is an organic process, inextricably linked to the roles, responsibilities and reflections at the heart of leading practice. As a result, chapters are interrelated. In each there is sustained 'mapping' – both forward and back – to the contributions made by each part of the writing team as we aim to illustrate the features and considerations required in this practice-focused approach to research. We would hope that this represents the spiral of reflection and action characteristic of critically reflective practice and demonstrates the interconnectedness of the various elements of a research project. It is particularly informed by the work of Oancea and Pring (2008) and their discussion of academic rigour and thoroughness in education research, as well as of Costley and Armsby (2007).

Organisation of the book

The book is organised into three sections:

- *purpose and approaches to enquiry* (Planning for Research);

- *exploring critical thinking in action* (Carrying Out Research);

- *continuing professional development* (Learning from Research).

Chapter 1 looks at 'ethics' first and foremost as part of daily practice in leading and managing teams. This is extended to identify how principles and protocols familiar to practitioners are reflected in research processes. The protection of participants – children and adults alike – is discussed and illustrated through the reflections of experienced practitioners. The chapter establishes some principles which are given further consideration by successive chapters and then reflected within the discussion in Chapter 8 of a framework for ethical conduct.

The aim of Chapter 2 is to open up for practitioners the idea of what research involves, to make it accessible by relating unconscious/intuitive aspects of daily practice to relevant, academic terminology. The chapter itself exposes the author's values and beliefs, based on experience and her own research heritage. It identifies her 'position' and allows us to hear an alternative perspective on practice-based research. In so doing, the chapter encourages a debate about the very nature of investigative work. It challenges 'orthodoxy' and asks that we listen carefully to the voices of those most closely involved, which is the underlying message in this book.

Chapter 3 discusses ethnography as representative of a particular feature of methodology. Through the exploration of a particular case study, it demonstrates the ways in which this 'methodology' lends itself to small-scale work-based research undertaken by practitioners seeking a greater understanding of their practice through collaboration with, and representation of, those they seek to serve.

Chapter 4 considers the ways in which investigation of literature and 'expert opinion' informs practice and any local change initiatives as practitioners seek to improve provision. With examples from experiences as diverse as changing a biscuit at snack-time to conducting a formal undergraduate project, the authors demonstrate how all practice is informed by a wide range of source material. The chapter looks at how to locate and learn from large-scale formal research which informs the credibility of localised investigations, together with sources of evidence of good practice at a more practical level.

Chapter 5 extends the earlier discussion on 'methods' for investigation. The focus is on qualitative methods, with some discussion on the relative merits of approaches such as using surveys which tend to take the form of questionnaires. There is a particular focus on methods that facilitate the active involvement and sustained contributions of children and parents, with notes supported by contributions from experienced early years practitioners based upon their own investigations.

Chapter 6 draws on the perceptions and experiences of novice researchers as well as the reflections of practitioners about their work-based investigations. It considers what 'data' are and how they can be used and interrogated to produce a coherent, reliable and authentic view of practice. It offers guidance on the different ways that practitioners report and interpret their findings. It shows that data are part of the whole process of an investigation. It looks at what cautionary checks might be made on the data to ensure they are fit for purpose.

Chapter 7 explores the impact of investigation on practitioners and practice. It examines critical thinking as part of professional development and change. The chapter examines the personal professional development that can result from learning through localised research, and the development of teams/settings as a consequence of engagement with reflective practice. There are illustrative contributions from practitioners.

Chapter 8 has 'emerged' from our research in developing this book. It is included primarily to show the importance of a coherent ethical framework as the basis for research/investigation in early years settings. Our research activities involved investigating research evidence, interrogating the literature and deliberately seeking out materials that informed and challenged research in practice. The work of the authors in this chapter does just that. In a quite accessible way they consider the component parts of an ethical framework in order to suggest a working model that other practitioners can adapt for local contexts. We have shared this with many practitioners and students who have all remarked how useful it is to them as researchers and as practitioners who wish to inform and lead others in their settings. Indeed, it has moved some to use this framework as the basis to review their own policies about the ethical protocols for students and others engaged in any form of investigation in their settings.

Further reading

These are suggested at the end of most chapters. These may be informed by texts featured by each contributor or presented as an opportunity to extend your understanding of key themes and concepts by investigating some new material – much of which is significant to the current discourse (body of knowledge and thinking) about research. In this way, we hope to scaffold your research skills and enhance use of the digital landscape. Chapter 8 is presented with a comprehensive, annotated source list as recommended by the authors. In some cases this duplicates items on the academic source list for the book, but all references utilised by the writing team are presented, in line with convention, as a listing at the back of the book.

To get you started

There are a number of 'sister' publications used in this text as source references for developing details of research which we outline in the context of our discussion of quality improvement and reflective practice. These are:

Costley, C., Elliott, G. and Gibbs, P. (2010) *Doing Work-Based Research*. London: Sage.
Denscombe, M. (2010) *The Good Research Guide for Small-Scale Social Research Projects*, 4th edn. Buckingham: Open University Press.

In addition, students undertaking final-year degree projects or postgraduate investigations will find further theoretical detail in:

Somekh, B. and Lewin, C. (2005) *Research Methods in Social Sciences*. London: Sage.

A number of online resources are also recommended.

An exploration of the three key themes of our text and a useful summary regarding these issues for others who are new to this field may be found at:

Hatten, R., Knapp, D. and Salonga, R. (1997) Action Research: Comparison with the concepts of 'The Reflective Practitioner' and 'Quality Assurance'. Online at: http://www.scu.edu.au/schools/gcm/ar/arr/arow/rdr.html.

Available online from Sage Publications is a variety of video lectures that are most useful for understanding aspects of research. They are streamed via YouTube:

SAGE Research Methods Online: An Introduction. Uploaded by Sage Publications to http://youtube.com.

The following site is worth looking at and tells you about Sage's Little Green Books which are practical aids to research:

http://www.methodspace.com/profiles/blogs/sages-little-green-books.

The following site is a good introduction to some of the key terms and concepts in education. It is mainly designed for students on education courses but should also be useful for others with an interest in education.

Gillies, D., *A Brief Critical Dictionary of Education*. Online at: http://dictionaryofeducation.co.uk/Complete.aspx.

Section 1

Planning for Research

1

Ethical positioning in work-based investigations

Sue Callan with Linda Picken and Sue Foster

Chapter overview

This chapter discusses the respectful practices at the heart of early years provision. These echo established ethical guidelines relating to the conduct of professional enquiry by practitioners. We argue that the kind of work-based investigation most usually involved in leading and managing teams arises from day-to-day reflective practice, as experienced practitioners seek to continuously improve work with children and families. As a result, we present an exploration of ethics in the context of daily practice. We seek to show that the 'academic' preoccupation with formal processes outlined in Chapter 2 offers a useful framework for ensuring that 'real-world'/insider research is conducted in an appropriately professional manner. So, while we illustrate our discussion with pictures from undergraduate academic projects, we do so as part of the scheme of the text overall – to apply direct experience from practice in order to illustrate complex academic concepts. We reflect on our experience as experienced practitioners in England and the small-scale investigations that have enhanced our ability to make an impact on practice – including the awareness of decisions relating to leadership and conscious, ethical management of settings and people.

In the UK, the BERA (2004, online) guidelines are a recognised point of reference for informing ethical decisions about 'formal' research projects. The Scottish guidelines are featured in our end-of-chapter activities. While these apply to all major, funded research projects they are also a useful source for student researchers and practitioners wishing to adopt professional protocols, i.e. the things that everyone should do. Only Scandinavia and Australia have *laws* appertaining to ethical research. Early Childhood Australia's Code of Ethics (2010, online) reflects these statutory requirements and therefore highlights children's well-being as paramount and that 'research' includes routine documentation of learning and development. Similarly, we note here (but expand in Chapter 8) how our consideration of ethics in practice has been enhanced by the work of Cullen et al. (2009) in New Zealand. In a very accessible paper, Dockett et al. (2009) have shown how these principles can be effectively applied, supporting our view that ethical practice underpins pedagogy, leadership and management responsibility and influencing our selection of headings within this chapter. The Australian ethical code also requires 'researchers' to make informed decisions about the participation of all concerned based on a clear understanding of the *purpose* and value of the proposed investigation.

The chapter offers a practical application of these key themes for colleagues aiming to inform their leadership through critically reflective work-based investigation. It is helpful to consider 'ethics' as the basis of a 'contract' for working with others, which includes:

- professional conduct and management of 'informal' investigation;

- protection of participants from 'harm';

- inclusion and diversity;

- the challenges of working with the Internet.

The chapter focuses on identifying strategies for the planning and conduct of work-based enquiry and a clear framework for this is offered in Chapter 8 which is a 'sister' chapter developing the discussion of ethical practice as it relates to reflection on action. We hope that the framework will work just as well for 'formal' academic projects as the professional management of 'informal' investigations conducted as part of leadership actions.

General context

If you are an early childhood practitioner working with children and families, ethical responsibilities are at the very heart of your role. You will be familiar with the requirements of the Data Protection Act 1998 (online) with the focus on privacy, anonymity and confidentiality. You will be well aware of the values and attitudes underpinning anti-discriminatory practice in the setting and for promoting inclusion. You will be leading and managing others to ensure that the welfare requirements of the Early Years Foundation Stage (EYFS, in England) (DCSF, 2008a) or relevant national frameworks are met with regard to child-centred practice and human rights legislation. These are all working examples of ethical management as discussed in Robins and Callan (2009).

In terms of the responsibility for implementing the EYFS (or national variation), your work will also be informed by personal and professional values which are reflected in the themes and principles underpinning early childhood policy objectives such as Every Child Matters (DfES, 2004). Canning (2009) discusses values-based leadership as it applies theory and philosophies of the early childhood tradition. A cycle of reflection (Appleby, 2010) will inform your practice overall – underpinned by commitment to the collaborative approaches expected of Early Years Professionals (EYP) in England (CWDC, 2009), and for all those leading practice in the four nations of the UK as illustrated in Chapter 4. Such an approach also needs to take heed of ethical guidelines in order to ensure that practice values are consistently applied. When we work with those closest to us (in 'insider' research), it is easy to assume that the quality of day-to-day relationships will carry through intuitively into such projects. To be an ethical manager and researcher continued vigilance is needed to ensure that such assumptions do not lead to oversight and misrepresentation of those involved. In short, ethical approaches mean that you will be aware of your position as researcher and how this affects the investigation. In daily practice, these ethical commitments, represent a way of 'being' just as the habit of reflection becomes a part of the professional qualities of experienced practitioners. We recommend the work of Newman and Pollnitz (2002) for their effective visual representation of this way of 'being' and much of this chapter is represented in their 'ethical response cycle'. Similarly, Alderson and Morrow (2011) discuss the role and position of the researcher, with additional material on assessing harm and benefits to participants.

Professional propriety – planning and managing a process

The work-based investigations featured in this chapter were under-taken as a personal, professional enquiry into the development of practice by experienced practitioners engaged in academic professional development. However, each was centred on a perceived 'problem' for practice in the workplace – with the purpose of understanding and resolving challenges to facilitate positive change. As such the examples are characteristic of the informal investigations common in settings. In this first picture from practice, Linda shows how ethical issues informed her initial plan of action in embracing change for the setting.

> For my work-based investigation I chose to re-examine my interpretation of the Reggio Emilia approach to learning. My concern for practice was that we had adopted the philosophies and values from Reggio as the result of research and ... I wanted to be assured that our principles could work successfully with the EYFS framework (DCSF, 2008a). I planned to read and update myself in terms of literature concerning the early years curriculum frameworks, but I also identified how I was going to share this opportunity for reflection in our 'community'. I aimed to hold focus group sessions with practitioners within my setting. The views of the parents also held significant value and I wanted the children to be given the opportunity to voice their views. In order to do this, I sought permission from the Centre management group to proceed and then permission from every practitioner willing to help. I had to inform every one verbally of my intentions, and then issue a consent letter to those practitioners who expressed a willingness to contribute. The same principle of choice applied to the parents. To safeguard the children I needed parental permission – I sent out a letter seeking permission and explaining how I would ensure anonymity for all participants when 'publishing' my final report. I also had to be clear in indicating the other professionals (tutors and manager) who would see the data, and my finished report. (Adapted from Picken, unpublished 2007)

There are a number of features in this account, not least a willingness to review local core principles in advance of externally driven change. Firstly, the investigation is reflexive in terms of the levels of reflective practice represented by Newman and Pollnitz's (2002) ethical response cycle – Linda is conducting a critical review of her own values and practice as part of a process of change. In addition, this account of planning for her investigation covers a range of expected professional proprieties:

- obtaining approval from management committees/authorities;

- obtaining consent/permissions from participants and their representatives;

- publicising procedure and principles so that there is 'transparency' in the investigation;

- informing those involved of their rights – there is choice offered in terms of participation;

- indicating the process for reporting or publishing the details of the investigation. In this case, the work was undertaken and published as part of a course. For practitioner investigations it is not unusual to share findings and experiences in a wider local network. *Provided all ethical considerations have been followed at the time*, your work should not be subject to veto or challenge at a later date;

- obtaining explicit authorisation for observation and visual data, the examination of files and records and the use of direct quotations from focus groups, also a feature of best practice.

These management action points relate to key themes for ethical practice which are developed below. Professional friends and mentors can offer support as your investigation progresses – at least to apply rigour to your ethical decisions. This strategy enables reflection in process so professional colleagues can also be involved in shaping the study and is illustrated in Figure 7.1 in Chapter 7.

Protecting others from harm – care for yourself and others

The summary by Plymouth Area Safeguarding Board of a Serious Case Review into incidents in a local nursery (2010, online) reveals, among many concerns, that practitioners in the setting lacked awareness of ethical propriety. The principle of ethical practice is fundamental to work with children and families yet is rarely made a conscious part of setting reflection. No doubt the framework outlined by our colleagues in Chapter 8 will inform and extend the awareness of leaders and managers to this area of self-appraisal and review, but it is invaluable for framing consideration of the 'balance of power' in investigations.

In formulating a plan for any investigation, you should also be sensitive to the context of your practice and the duties to protect from harm both children and vulnerable adults. Let us take the example of multi-agency settings as discussed by Whitmarsh (2007), and in particular the notion of ethical codes for work-based investigation as part of local policy. She notes that a national 'one-size fits all' notion of a research code of ethics may not be the solution to concern for protecting children and families as participants. We note that practitioners in children's centres may be working with many families who have been referred by social and care services. Some parents in this situation may well have mental health issues or be affected by the effects of social deprivation. Callan and Morrall (2009) argue that this does not mean that children and families are not competent and cannot exercise agency in terms of participation – indeed the families are representing social groups conventionally without a 'voice' as the result of isolation. However, while maintaining early years pedagogical principles of competency and agency, sensitive researchers need to be aware of the potential and actual vulnerability of participants of all ages. This involves careful reflection, as the longer-term implication of your proposed actions may not be immediately apparent. It is better to assume that all participants are *potentially* vulnerable in order to consider your assumptions and plan the conduct of the study. These ideas are extended here in relation to a second working example which 'revealed' power dynamics to the researcher.

Power and emotional literacy

For many managers and leaders, it may be useful to consider participant 'vulnerability' in terms of the balance of power in relationships within any investigation. This also requires a degree of emotional literacy (Pilcher, 2009) as it is recognised by Opie that informed consent of participants can have the institutional effect of 'absolving the researcher of their moral and ethical responsibility' (2004: 28). The following reflection on a practitioner investigation provides a working example of this concept in terms of work with adult colleagues. Here, Sue Foster is reflecting on the power and emotional dimensions of her research as an owner/manager.

> My investigation focused on developing outdoor provision in the Nursery. Really, it was an extension of an earlier study (Foster, 2006) where I concluded that as a team we needed a much more reflective approach to practice. I was trying to facilitate reflection in the context of developing our outdoor classroom and did so in a series of focus groups and workshops. Several of the staff mentioned their unpleasant school experiences and seemed wary, even nervous of what was going to be expected of them. I also felt on many occasions that there was an expectation that I would transmit all the information and

that staff were passive rather than active, interested participants. As a result, I found it difficult to resist 'teaching' what I felt the participants needed to know. The barrier of participant's values and staff hierarchy did arise and I found all this quite frustrating.

I realise that my expectations must have weighed very heavily on my staff. The targets I had in mind at the outset have now become a longer journey. However, I do feel that we took the first steps towards that goal. (Adapted from Foster, unpublished 2008)

Note how participation in research for colleagues in the closest and most successful teams can be a stressful experience. The team felt vulnerable, despite the careful attention to ethical protocol involved in the planning process, and this vulnerability extended to the leader.

Sharing experiences – how can I protect the well-being of participants?

Focus group discussions can involve sharing sensitive personal information at times and this could be upsetting for some members – the very opposite of the empowering outcome you will have planned. When planning your strategies, consider whether you enable the participants to control the extent of the personal information disclosed. Advice in terms of ethicality is to allow time to 'debrief' and make sure everyone is 'okay' (reflecting on the reflection) before disbanding. When writing up the discussion (the point at which it becomes your 'data'), very powerful responses can be identified and it is useful to revisit individually with some participants their choice to continue or not. For this reason, a research journal is vital for recording, planning and managing a work-based investigation. Journalising is a useful tool in its own right, shown by Mukherji and Albon (2010) as part of critical reflective practice.

In the same vein, be careful that in written accounts of activities, the same respectful concern is shown for the sensitivities of participants. When representing real conversations, ensure that their voices are 'authentic' in the reports. This will involve making a distinction between their voices and your own in writing up activities. In asking for verification of the experience from the group, they will have control over the record of their own conversation. While the reflection and interpretation may be your own, ensure that it is based on a proper understanding of the meanings intended by the group. Thus the core participant group might receive full 'reports' of the activities, having access to your own reflections and the progress of the study.

Through these techniques it is possible to demonstrate sensitivity to the people involved, as well as to decisions about the research process itself. In work-based practice it is hard to differentiate between a role as participant observer (insider) and the need to be an 'outsider' at the point of analysing data. Hitchcock and Hughes propose that 'teacher-researchers need, therefore, to be aware of the two roles that participant observation involves and be able to overcome any conflict during the research process by adopting as open an approach as possible' (1995: 48). Sharon Smith discusses how ethical issues extend to the use of and interpretation of data in Chapter 6.

This picture from practice offers further action points related to ethical planning. Building on the initial protocols of consultation, negotiation and consent, we can add the following:

- Involve stakeholders from the outset in the practice outcome that you envisage in order to shape the form of the study.

- Take account of the wishes of others concerning the level of their involvement. (In Sue Foster's experience there was a worry about activities requiring a degree of literacy. Offer alternatives – see Chapter 5 on creative approaches to methods.)

- Take care to exercise some emotional sensitivity concerning the conduct of your enquiry and identify support if needed for participants.

- Allow 'dissent' – participants may withdraw or challenge your interpretation.

- Ensure 'participant validation' which involves enabling your respondents to 'check' your descriptions and interpretation of their work/words for fairness and accuracy.

- Be sensitive to the nature of your 'reports' and dissemination of findings – different audiences may require different styles of presentation.

- Finally, make it clear what will happen to your data at the end of the study. There should be no need to keep materials beyond the life of the investigation.

Flewitt (2005) constructs a discussion about ethics on the notion of 'sharing' as it informs and underpins the research process. This is a feature characteristic of the work-based investigations featured in this text, and the notion of shared lives and stories offered by the approaches to investigations promoted in Chapter 3. As a researcher, recognising that you are part of a sharing *community* rather than a project leader will help form an ability to address the power balance apparent in professional hierarchies. It will also engage with the concept of communities of practice discussed in Chapter 7.

Care for yourself

To finalise this section, in which we have explored the notion of 'protection from harm', it is important to recognise that an ethical approach should also extend to consideration of *yourself*. For example, on a practical level, Mukherji and Albon (2010) note the importance of personal safety as part of your ethical responsibilities. While you will be motivated to ensure your participants are as comfortable as possible in your study, when collecting individual responses you are advised to be aware of your own potential vulnerability if visiting (for example) private accommodation. This point may also lead you to reflect on how to maintain professional relationships within an inclusive approach to management of practice.

Work with young children and families is challenging and demanding. Care for yourself enables you to conserve energy in a situation where the demands of the job involve consistently giving energy away – to your team, to the children and to families (Robins and Callan, 2009). Aubrey et al. (2000) remind us that it is important to extend the same concern to yourself and your 'supporters'. It is imperative not to neglect personal relationships in the process of your work and research. At the very least, keep in mind that as an early years practitioner you should 'practise what you preach'.

Inclusion and diversity – meaningful participation for children and adults

The strategies outlined above demonstrate an ethical approach in that they are representative of respectful practice. In constructing plans for investigation, practitioners will give due regard to the factors that inhibit or enhance the involvement of participants – we have noted considerations of time and personal/social contexts in particular. These issues can also be extended to consideration of the purpose and nature of involvement and from there to ensuring inclusive approaches.

It is respectful of children and families to consider whether their participation is strictly necessary at every part of the investigation – as this reflection on the development of Linda's (Picken, unpublished 2007) original research plan demonstrates. Here we can see how she moved from a plan involving a fairly superficial 'consultation' exercise to consideration of more meaningful involvement at a later stage of an evolving enquiry – an example clearly representative of the Early Childhood Australia ethical code (2010, online).

> The focus group helped to give the study validity; it helped create data, which was valid in supporting our reflection on values and assisting decisions about the future evolution of our practice for implementing the EYFS. The focus groups also occurred in parallel to my continued reading/literature exploration, shared with professional colleagues in the local authority – including the practice improvement team for early years. In the course of this process, I recognised that, whilst the children were going to be the primary end users of our provision, given the evolution of the investigation, it would have been difficult to directly involve them at this stage in any meaningful way. In making this a practitioner-focussed study, I did not overlook the need for some triangulation. As the study evolved, this changed from the stakeholders in the setting, to some colleagues from my team, involvement of outside professionals and local agencies and my independent review of expert opinion through literature search. I can see that this was far more relevant to the stage of our reflection than my original action plan. Once we had received our training about the EYFS from the local authority and were more aware of the expectations placed upon us, parents and children were involved in evaluation of our provision as we worked together to embed the new requirements. (Adapted from Picken, unpublished 2007)

We can see from this example that allowing time to clarify the purpose of involvement for the participants can offer focus to your selection of methods in a continuing spiral of reflection. Once this is apparent, a sensitive approach to diversity is essential. For example, bilingual colleagues may facilitate the involvement of children and parents with English as an additional language, either by directly translating conversation or offering dual-language presentation of questionnaires. Naturally, you will need to include colleagues in ethical discussion about confidentiality of data and acknowledge their involvement in terms of parental consent and permissions. Your focus in planning your investigation will be primarily informed by professional principles and a consideration of how to involve other participants with specific needs – literacy having been noted in the examples above. The work of Rose Drury

(2007) is a good reference point and source of information for inclusive strategies.

Selecting appropriate methods – principles for active participation and well-being

It is clear that some strategies for research with young children enable an inclusive approach so that even the youngest, pre-verbal children will have a 'voice' in your investigations. As a result of continuing professional development activities, experienced practitioners should be aware of the Mosaic approach, in which Alison Clark (2004) has proposed a selection of child-centred strategies in a research 'toolkit' (as explored in Chapters 3 and 5). These strategies are particularly relevant to work-based investigations since many projects centre on improving the child's experience in practice. In terms of ethics, the approach is consistent with rights-based practice and EYFS (DCSF, 2008a) principles of listening to children. Clark's tools provide children with agency and real involvement rather than a superficial consultation based on (say) 'interviews' formulated to suit an adult 'agenda'. Mukherji and Albon (2010) note that traditional methods such as observation are vital to carrying out research with very young children and babies – and employing interview techniques continues to be useful, providing that the children are able to participate. At a practical level, if we apply our knowledge of theory to research planning, we can identify that the Mosaic approach suits children as participants because it involves their active participation and consideration of their expressed views (or behavioural responses) in constructing a shared understanding of our environment. In terms of the philosophies informing current practice, we can see that the Mosaic methods value the creativity and imagination of children.

For work with children, Alderson (2005) proposes that we adopt an ethical stance that is based on the notion that involvement will be based on their interests and level of knowledge and understanding. This highlights what they know and can do rather than presenting a situation that is difficult for them. In consideration of strategies for inclusion, we need to evaluate our research planning on the basis of these values to ensure that children are empowered in the investigation – they can exercise *choice*. This approach will apply to other groups of participants who may traditionally be 'hard to engage' (see Chapter 3), but for all participants we must aim to ensure:

- meaningful inclusion on the basis of access, language, literacy and culture;

- involvement linked to their real, rather than perceived, interests and knowledge;

- an experience that provides a situation that is affirming of their abilities, sensitive to their needs and respects their expertise with regard to their own experiences.

Overall, it is worth considering your responsibility to respond to the needs of the children while you are undertaking research activities such as video recording and observations. These methods are recognised as 'naturalistic' in terms of the Mosaic approach and can be interpreted for your findings. However, you should be clear that, when observing children as part of daily practice, it is necessary to exercise some sensitivity to a child's feelings at that particular time. You will make decisions about whether it is 'fair' to continue your observation if (say) the child appears to be overly tired. In research practice involving children or participants with specific needs who may be unable to articulate their own anxieties, the professional duty to protect their interests must remain central to your conduct. There may well be a tension between the time frame for your investigation and the recognition that 'now' is not a 'good time', but you will always strive to act ethically. 'Tuning in' to the children's mood can help you overcome the conflict that may occur between concepts of 'participant consent', and 'agreement' that have to be maintained over a longitudinal study. At the very least, bear in mind that when parents *consent* to their child's involvement, their *agreement* is based on the expectation that you will be responsible for the child's well-being during the actual research activity in their absence.

The challenges of working with the Internet

In ethical terms, use of the Web and ICT tools presents challenges for exercising personal integrity in keeping to your research 'contract'. However, in practice, providers of children's services are increasingly turning to such technology as part of managing parent expectations and communication. For example, the use of a webcam, text messaging and web pages for information about the setting all promote access and involvement of parents and carers, but leaders have had to deal sensitively with the ethical issues involved, the more so given the outcomes of the Plymouth review (Plymouth Safeguarding Board, 2010, online). Similarly, it is important to consider visual data (observations, video/recording equipment and photographs) as part of the same ethical approach. While Mukherji and Albon (2010) offer a sound overview of such methods, it is made clear that ethical deliberations will include specific, informed consent for such recording – including details of who will see it, secure storage and how long the material will be kept. Recent high-profile legal cases in England (Plymouth Safeguarding Board, 2010, online) have highlighted the concern about the Internet and safeguarding issues, so practitioners need to be aware of any local authority guidelines in this respect and honour these in formulating a plan for investigation.

In researching practice, some leaders have effectively employed the professional networks to be found through the Internet, so it is important to consider web-based conferencing in this context. While the basic protocols outlined throughout the chapter all apply, Eysenbach and Till (2001) demonstrate that there are issues specific to Internet research for consideration. Use of the World Wide Web raises particular questions about informed consent and confidentiality – mainly because it is possible to study the information and discussion groups as an observer and not 'announce' yourself or your intentions to participants. Similarly, it is possible to participate in communication without announcing your motivation and intention to use content – yet it can be complex to engage in traditional research approaches where the researcher is identified and utilising online interviews, focus groups or surveys.

At this point it is easy to understand why key themes of anonymity and confidentiality in relation to specific research methods are regarded by Flewitt (2005) as an ethical minefield. Internet users do not necessarily expect to be research subjects, and although they inhabit a public space, they are very much located in the privacy of their own context which can impact on the understanding of 'consent' and issues of 'validation' discussed in Chapter 2. Denscombe (2010) also recognises the need to appreciate the limitations of confidentiality and privacy when using the Internet. O'Dochartaigh (2002) reinforces this point by reminding us that there is technology to allow agencies for security and policing to trace the origins of any Internet communication to source if they so wish. Put simply, it is impossible to guarantee anonymity and confidentiality in this context.

However, we would encourage practitioners to engage in the digital landscape as part of their developing practice and, for advice on using this medium for research, the recent work of Ford (2011) is particularly useful.

The following example shows how one experienced practitioner worked to resolve these difficulties in an investigation utilising the Internet community of parents engaged in the evolution of 'baby signing' as part of language development.

Professional propriety

> Posting an open message on the relevant network site facilitated explanation of the research agenda and personal interests. It gave the opportunity for interested individuals to volunteer, to gain further information and to 'opt in' to the study. 'Formal' permission was then obtained from those individuals, who then contributed to the study through shared personal experiences and the electronic completion of a questionnaire. Undertakings about debriefing at the end of the study and data storage/disposal were provided at the initial stage of gaining consent.

Protection from harm

> Participant details were kept confidential in reporting the study. Material and contact was made only through public sites or from individuals aware of the research agenda. Note that in small-scale work-based investigations the data gathered would not be in the public domain. It was still necessary to consider 'protection' issues in order to decide what to leave out when presenting findings in the final report.

Transparency

> As this practitioner was also using case study/significant incident recording of her own child's communication strategies, she was personally positioned in the centre of the project. She had to be clear when she was collecting data and record a commitment to fair representation of findings (rather than just things that agreed with her own perspective).

The key to the effectiveness of this study lay in careful planning and research around ethical issues for the particular context involved and discussing strategies with professional critical friends – a process applicable in all situations.

Summary

We have stressed that issues of ethicality are aligned with trustful relationships in open, honest communication – a professional way of 'being'. Such transparency is a professional principle for work in early years, but it is also a mindset that informs the professional management of workplace investigation. Whether an investigation is 'informal' (remaining within the confines of the setting) or the subject of formal report as a small-scale academic project, the decisions and practices relating to ethicality will determine the credibility of outcome for future practice. 'Ethics' is concerned with far more than issues of 'anonymity' and 'confidentiality', as is detailed in Chapter 8. Close attention to ethical issues will inform your development as an ethical leader/manager, a reflective practitioner and a critical researcher. We show in Chapter 7 that practitioner investigation will contribute to professional knowledge, enhance the quality of provision and offer the opportunity for communities in practice to share an affirming experience. As personal, professional development, it enables practitioners to contribute to wider networks and discourses about 'quality' on the basis of informed, grounded and critical reflective practice.

Further reading

The following text seems to us to be very contemporary and further investigation of the chapters on 'Researchers as Insiders or Outsiders' and 'Assessing Harms and Benefits' would be useful:

Alderson, P. and Morrow, V. (2011) *The Ethics of Research with Children and Young People: A Practical Handbook*. London: Sage.

For an exploration of the various guidelines to ethical practice see the following online sources. It should be possible to identify how these frameworks have informed our chapter.

Scottish Educational Research Association (SERA) (2005) *Ethical Guidelines for Educational Research*. Online at: http://www.sera.ac.uk.
British Educational Research Association (BERA) (2004) *Revised Ethical Guidelines for Educational Research*. Southwell. Online at: http://www.bera.ac.uk/.
American Educational Research Association (AERA) (2000) *Ethical Standards of AERA*. Online at: http://www.aera.net/about/policy/ethics.htm.

2

Expressing personal values and beliefs – the essential position of the researcher

Carla Solvason

Chapter overview

This chapter is presented as a critical response to the way in which students and practitioners are introduced to 'research' in higher education programmes. It questions the relevance of existing institutional frameworks (or discourses) to practitioner investigations. By exploring values and beliefs, experience, actions and research heritage, this chapter examines for the novice researcher an understanding of what 'research' involves and makes it accessible – by challenging the excess of academic terminology and relating the intuitive aspects of daily life to the processes involved. It also provides a model of critical analysis for inexperienced writers, representing a position resulting from reflection on established theory, professional experience and values. It invites the reader to make a personal response, thereby promoting the critical reflective practice which lies at the heart of finding one's own 'methodological position'.

My views on practitioner research within the early years have been developed recently through working with students at university.

Increasingly I have become frustrated by the convoluted and complex way that research is often introduced making it inaccessible to many. Within this chapter I would like to make clear that research plays a part in every aspect of your career path and that it is far more straightforward than many of you have been led to believe. First it will be useful to clarify what I mean by the terms 'research' and 'research methods'. Contrary to the presumption that research has to be a complex scientific experiment, research is, in actuality, making a concerted effort to look into a topic. And on this basis I defy anyone reading this book to claim that they have never done research: whether it was about your next hairstyle or a new loft conversion, you have all looked up information on a topic. You have found information on the Internet, chatted to friends, gained the advice of experts – so you are not completely new to the idea, although you may have been led to believe that you are. While searching for that information, what methods did you use? Did you read books, websites, articles in newspapers and magazines? Did you catch up with old friends that you knew were familiar with the subject? These all comprised your research methods. Research is something that we do day to day and not something reserved only for academic types. In this chapter I hope to convince you that research is a facet of your everyday practice and that a research project is simply a more refined way of exploring a topic.

Firstly, let us be clear that there is nothing 'mystical' about research; it really is just a more systematic way of investigating an issue. Secondly, with research you are venturing into the unknown. There is no tried and tested way of doing a piece of research. If it has already been done then there is no point doing it again. Each and every piece of research is unique – a different approach, a different setting, different people – which is what makes it exciting. There is no right or wrong answer if no two pieces of research are the same, neither is there one accepted approach. It is an experiment – you try it out and see how it goes. As Phillips and Pugh rationalise it: 'You are not doing research in order to do research; you are doing research in order to demonstrate that you have learned *how* to do research …' (1994: 20). No one can expect you to do something perfectly on your first attempt.

Whether we are aware of it or not, research is an inherent element of our practice in early years. In order to be recognised as professionals, we need to show pride in the fact that we are researchers. As Hedges notes, we need to recognise the extent to which 'practitioner research contributes to the knowledge base of education' (2001: 2) and ignore the tendency to presume that this type of research is lower in status than university-based research. Safford and Hancock compare 'big science' (2010: 8) with small-scale practice research. I would agree with their challenge to the assumption that 'big science' research is of greater value than practice-based research, as it is the small-scale investigation that influences day-to-day practice. Now I am not suggesting that all early years practitioners walk around carrying clipboards, glasses perched on the ends of their noses, making copious notes. Ours is a practical approach to research: we constantly reflect on and modify our practice – and this is central to what we do. For some reason, far too many early years colleagues appear to have bought into the fallacy that research is for academics and not for us mere mortals. Somehow the concept of research has taken on gargantuan proportions so that it invokes terror in the undergraduate and is viewed as something that is accessible only to the intellectually gifted. In this chapter I would like to dispel this ridiculous myth. Research is as relevant to early years as it is to any other phase, and it is far more straightforward than the harbingers of paradigms and 'ologies' would have you believe. There are only two vital ingredients to producing a piece of research: *purpose* and *ethicality*.

Ethicality in research

You will notice that ethicality appears a number of times within this text, but I raise only a few points here. A problem that regularly occurs when students focus on a research topic is that they will choose a subject that they are intensely interested in but forget how inextricably linked that is with the child's upbringing. And although we should be working closely with families we cannot, as outsiders, be telling parents and carers how they should be raising their children. I will give as an example of this some students' fascination with children's healthy eating. Although it is important that we promote healthy eating within settings, students have a tendency to go about this topic in a largely critical way. What, exactly, can we glean from monitoring children's lunchboxes other than to criticise families for not feeding their children healthily enough? As practitioners we need to carefully consider the level of care that we are providing rather than judging others. Ways to encourage young children to eat more healthily would be an extremely worthwhile investigation;

criticising the foods that parents prepare for their children is not. It is far more productive for us to first look at things that *we* can improve rather than seeking to improve others. Avoiding any tendency to judge and being conscious of our own subjective viewpoint is central to the development of our research topic and will help us to ensure that we are taking an ethical approach.

There is far more to say on ethicality and it is explored more fully in other chapters. As is shown in Chapter 1, if you ensure that you always gain permission from carers and from managers for your research, if you ensure that no children are being advantaged or disadvantaged by your research but that there is parity of experience, if you ensure that the participants are able to opt in and out of the research and if you ensure that all data is anonymised and confidential, then you are off to a good start. Always consider, 'is it possible that I could upset or offend anyone with this research?' If the answer is 'yes', then you may do well to explore a different avenue, at least at this point in you career. There is a wealth of information available on approaching research ethically that is worth reviewing. Two particularly recent and useful examples are Costley et al. (2010) and Mukherji and Albon (2010). In addition Helen Hedges (2001) discusses your dual responsibility as both practitioner and researcher and how your responsibilities as practitioner should come first.

Purpose and transparency in research

Above and beyond any amount of research knowledge, it is vital that students have a rational and purposeful basis for their research. Although seeing how long the 'average' two-year-old girl can stand on one foot may be something that is manageable and measurable (although the use of the word 'average' may take some clarifying), what possible purpose could there be for such research? Central to all early years research is the fundamental aim to improve the experience for children and families. We must be clear on exactly why we think that a piece of research is important. We must have carefully considered how it will enrich our knowledge of working with children and families. The *why* of the research is vital.

Most of the practitioner research that you will be engaged in will be work-based. It will either lead to a different way of doing things or a different way of seeing things. In the following chapter, Cooper and Ellis demonstrate how research is about seeing the familiar and new in a different way and honing the skills of critical analysis and reflection. As much as research is about the subject it is also about *you*. Your experiences and beliefs are inextricably entwined within your piece of research. As Atkinson and Hammersley point out: 'there is no perfectly transparent, or neutral, way to represent the natural or social world' (1994: 254). As a result, it is vital that you present your reasoning behind the research. Why have you chosen to do this research, what are the life experiences that have brought you to this point? If you choose to look into children's diet you need to make clear why this area is important to you. You need to make clear what you have read and found out about the subject, but also what has been your own lived experience, as child, parent or practitioner.

Le Gallais explores how challenging the concept of objectivity can be for researchers and notes how: 'Our experiences and the meanings we attribute to them are shaped by our backgrounds ... the culture(s), in which we function, and the people, with whom we interact' (2003: 2). The fact is that you, as researcher, will inevitably leave your 'prints' on the research, so it is vital that you are open and transparent about your beliefs surrounding the investigation. Before you embark on a study it is vital that you have considered your ethical and theoretical framework, and have reflected on how you reached the point of placing such importance on the topic that you are exploring. Before you begin to discuss *how* you carried out a piece of research, you must first explain your thinking – the *why*, a concept that is discussed in more detail in Chapter 4.

My own, large-scale research was into the development of specialist schools within the secondary system. I felt very strongly that it was unfair to elevate one skill over others and needed to take time to consider why. This became the 'theoretical framework' section of my thesis. In considering the strong feelings I had about the equality of educational experience, I had to acknowledge my own working-class background, my comprehensive education and my extensive work in schools in extremely underprivileged areas. These factors had a huge influence on what I considered to be 'fair' in terms of a child's educational choices and provision. I also needed to read extensively around the development of the specialist system and the concept of educational equality. When we embark on a discovery we need to be very clear about 'where we are coming from'.

Insider or outsider research?

Contrary to my own experience of carrying out research as an 'outsider' within the setting, many of you will be embarking on research within your own place of work. The concept of being an 'insider' or an 'outsider' when carrying out research is an extremely complex one. Some readily embrace the somewhat bizarre supposition that outsider researcher will be more rigorous. These are the types that will 'buy in' professional researchers, on, as Haviland et al. note, 'an assumption that only knowledge obtained objectively and systematically by external experts can offer valid and reliable evidence' (2005: 10). Contrary to this an outsider has no in-depth understanding of the culture of the settings that they are exploring. Hedges comments that 'a long-term relationship where the researcher knows participants well makes authenticity more likely' (2001: 2). Many of you, as practitioners researching within your own settings, will have such knowledge, but then this relationship can cause further complications. The concept of the insider/outsider researcher is not something that can be neatly packaged. Haviland et al. discuss how 'the position of insider/outsider is complex and multi-dimensional. Each of us can be insiders and outsiders in a particular community because we occupy multiple positions simultaneously' (2005: 13). We have pockets of experience and knowledge which are reliant on, and respond to, those with whom we work.

Can you choose whether to research as an insider or outsider and which is best? By accepting one's role as insider one forgoes those early attempts to become accustomed to a situation, as you are familiar with the intricate workings of your environment. And aren't most researchers striving to come to an in-depth understanding of a case when they embark on their study? So, one could safely assume that insider knowledge has its benefits. But Le Gallais (2003) issues a warning – based on her own research which took place in a school where she was employed – about the assumptions that can be made when we are overly familiar with a situation. She is critical of her own naivety in presuming that others would share her knowledge and imagining that 'the reality, which [she] inhabited was the same for all the participants' (2003: 5). With time, Le Gallais realised that there were others within her setting who had very different perceptions of the experience. In early years we are well aware that considering the differing views of others is part of the cycle of critical reflection.

Haviland et al. (2005) explore this within research and consider how important it is, when working very intimately within a situation, to be able to 'step back and reflect' upon one's own role and the processes that you, as a practitioner, are working within. They suggest that it is important, through critical analysis, 'to develop a more "outside perspective" as the danger is that through familiarity you will come to any situation with many preconceptions' (2005: 14).

During my own longitudinal research, although accepted by certain social groups within the setting, I essentially remained an outsider. As such I was tarred with the same brush as Ofsted inspectors, and practitioners' guards were continually up with regard to the information that they were willing to share with me. It took a very long time to earn the trust of those at the setting, but even then moments of honesty and openness from them only came with the assumption that I would, in fact, share the information with others. Phrases such as 'I don't care who hears it but ...' were not uncommon before the most controversial pieces of information were shared with me.

The role of the qualitative researcher is far more complex than many comprehend and involves far more facets of 'ethicality' than simply gaining parental permission. Punch discusses how central emotions can be to the research process:

> Entry and departure, distrust and confidence, elation and despondency, commitment and betrayal, friendship and abandonment – are all as fundamental here as dry discussions on the techniques of observation, taking field notes, analysing the data and writing the report. (1994: 84)

It is for these reasons that we need to become far more transparent about the problematic processes of practitioner research and disentangle them from the traditional shroud of mystery that has been placed around them. As tutors we expect students to go through a complex and, to some extent, emotionally loaded process, yet, for some reason we accept that concepts of research have been made as inaccessible as possible through a complex academic vocabulary. Students are expected to digest an unfamiliar language at the same time as beginning to understand how they can implement these concepts. If we are to empower early years practitioners within their research it is time that we reassessed the 'hows' and 'whys' of our approach.

Making research accessible to all

The longer that I work within the realm of early years care and education the more I come to believe that we are doing our students a disservice by attempting to shoehorn them into an academic discourse that is totally unsuited to their needs. The more I consider it, the more convinced I become that there is no possible reason for a second-year early years student to learn the term 'research paradigm'. I have to look up the meaning again every time I come across it, and still my interpretation will always differ from someone else's ... Let us instead start by using a language that is accessible to all. When a student embarks on research we should be asking: what do you want to find out? how will you go about it? what are you hoping to achieve? Isn't that more practical than discussing paradigms, methodologies and hypotheses?

I am unsure why early years researchers have bought into the academic tradition of giving a reasonably straightforward practice a new and obscure language. Within our realm of practice this simply does not apply. We are work-based practitioners, our study is purposeful, so we should not feel pressure to incorporate the pretensions of academia into our approach. I think it's about time that we chose to use research as a tool to fit our needs and not vice versa. Rather than drowning in 'ologies' we need to re-image research so that it can be useful to us. Instead of laboriously 'encouraging' students to grasp a new and mysterious language it is time that we encouraged them to tell us what they plan to investigate and how they plan to do it. It is quite possible that they would be able to explain why they chose the methods that they are using to collect the data, and why they are the best and most reliable methods, without once needing to utter a word ending in 'ology' or 'tative'. Indeed, these skills are apparent in successive contributions to this book from experienced practitioners.

Now, I know that there will be academic types out there 'tutting' accusingly at me for lowering standards or limiting expectations or something along those lines. But in response I would say that my focus is on that huge majority of early years practitioners working with children day to day who are educated to level 5 or 6 (i.e. they have completed a Foundation Degree or a BA). I refer to the practitioners who are doing most of the work and having most impact within settings, as indicated in the introduction to this book. There are students who show academic flair and interest in further study and they can be encouraged to extend and explore much as Jude Simms describes in Chapter 4. However, let us not confuse the students' desire to develop into more effective practitioners with a requirement for them to learn to speak in an obscure academic language that they will, in all likelihood, never, ever, use again.

The vast majority of 'research' that is continually happening within settings and benefitting our young children is 'useful' research that does not require a carefully constructed (and laboriously studied) research paradigm. It is organic. Every day practitioners are asking themselves questions about the learning and development of the children in their care, and every day they are trying out new methods to compare success. It is research, just not labelled as such. It seems that through our academic approach within further and higher education we are attempting to set 'research' up as a 'golden fleece', something all but unobtainable. By doing this we negate the value of the research that all of our students and practitioners take part in day to day. We are presenting research as a mystery to be gradually (and with a *lot* of hard work) discovered, when, in reality, it is an instinctive component of practitioner's daily interaction with the children. Holloway and Jefferson discuss how we use research skills every day without ever acknowledging them as such:

> In everyday informal dealings with each other, we do not take each other's accounts at face value, unless we are totally naïve; we question, disagree, bring in counter-examples, interpret, notice hidden agendas. Research is only a more formalised and systematic way of knowing about people ... (2000: 3)

And such 'knowing about people' takes far more subtlety and responsiveness than your average, pre-structured interview. Our aim, as early years practitioner-investigators, should be to find and refine ways to record this everyday thinking rather than to strive to grasp an elusive mystery.

Let us use this example. A group of students were introduced to the confusions of quantitative research. Having 'had a go' at creating a questionnaire in their first year, these students then discovered that this was not actually a questionnaire at all. It was made clear to them that written questions cannot, in fact, be called a questionnaire unless distributed to a sample no smaller than 3,700 and has previously been piloted by at least 85 people. Okay, I exaggerate a little, but you get the picture. The students were being told that what they had done had not actually been research at all, and in order to avoid their hard work being totally dismissed it could be given a new, qualitative title. If it was called a written interview rather than a questionnaire then that would be sufficient to prevent it from becoming the laughing stock of 'proper academics' the world over. The group were basically told, in not so many words, that quantitative research was far too complex for them to be attempting, and that if they stuck to the more 'wishy-washy' area of qualitative research they would be fine. The result was a group of entirely disheartened, and I would go so far as to say in some cases offended, students. It is ridiculous that we allowed this nonsensical monster of 'methodolatry' in to prey on student practitioners. Janesick uses the combination of methodology and idolatry to describe some academics' 'slavish attachment and devotion to method (which overshadows) the actual substance of the story being told' (1994: 215). Of course, there are different views about this within each and every department at any number of universities, but I suggest that we do not buy into such academic snobbery. Our discussions should be based around what the student wants to explore, which are the best and most appropriate methods with which to do that and whether they are fit for purpose.

Students cannot talk to every parent, so they write down their questions instead. Does it really matter whether this is referred to as a questionnaire or a written interview? So what? How is *x* number of questionnaires returned more valid than *y*? Surely we should be more concerned with the content than the number? If only ten questionnaires are returned, but three of them suggest real issues with a practice at the setting, then the findings are extremely *significant* (another loaded term in quantitative circles). Regardless of the small number, the results are significant with regard to the questions being asked. The questionnaire is fit for purpose.

Summary

Early years is a specialised field. Fleer is quite critical of the discourse and theoretical perspectives that have developed as a language of early childhood and suggests that Early Years practitioners have become enmeshed within a 'self-perpetuating set of values and practices that make it difficult to move thinking forward' (2003: 64). I could not disagree more. I have worked and studied within a range of fields and have never before worked with those who are as self-aware, reflective and forward-thinking as colleagues within the field of early years. It is

(Continued)

(Continued)

because of this questioning desire for self-improvement that research, as well as self-reflection, is inherent to the role of the early years practitioner. Those within the field are continually asking themselves not just 'how can I be better?', but also 'how can I do it better?' This is something that I hope I have done in this chapter as I have considered my own values and beliefs about engaging in research and considered current teaching strategies. Therefore in some ways I am entering into the discourse or body of knowledge surrounding the subject to prod and challenge what goes on.

Historically, early years is most definitely a field in which decisions have been 'done to' rather than 'made with'. It is important that as early years practitioners we make clear that we are capable researchers who have something to say about how things should be. This does not mean that we have to prostrate ourselves before existing research regimes, but that we should be more confident in developing our own approach. The more we are engaged in rigorous research that works, the more we should speak out about it. Goodfellow and Hedges comment that a 'critical way in which early childhood practitioners can be considered as professionals is for them to systematically engage in enquiry into their own practices' (2007: 187). It is not only in higher education or secondary education that practitioner research is taking place. We should be more willing to share the innovative ideas that are being explored day to day in early years' settings. It is time that we, as early childhood practitioners, embraced the Reggio Emilia approach to exploration, where research

> ... leaves – or rather, demands to come out of – the scientific laboratories, thus ceasing to be a privilege of the few (in universities and other designated places) to become the stance, the attitude with which teachers approach the sense and meaning of life. (Rinaldi, 2005: 148)

Further reading

Carla's chapter represents the considerable range of academic debate that contributes to our understanding of what is conventionally termed 'methodology'. It is important to see that Carla's position is informed by this debate and the chapter itself is a contribution to this 'discourse'. The sources below represent various positions in this discussion.

The interesting articles below by Hammersley and Hodkinson consider the rapid rise of a new educational research orthodoxy. Central to that orthodoxy are the assumptions that method can ensure objectivity in research, and that more objective 'safe' research to inform practice is needed. But educational research is a field made up of overlapping communities of practice. This field has rules, but they are largely unwritten, and modify and change as part of a contingent tradition. The authors suggest that research can only ever be partly rational and is related to developing researcher identities. It is suggested that research contributes to understanding in ways that owe more to the quality of interpretations of the data than to the objective purity of any methods used.

Hammersley, M. (2005) 'Countering the "new orthodoxy" in educational research; a response to Phil Hodkinson', *British Educational Research Journal*, 31 (2): 139–55.
Hodkinson, P. (2004) 'Research as a form of work: expertise, community and methodological objectivity', *British Educational Research Journal*, 30 (1): 9–26.

Drawing on an overview of the vast amount of documents expressing criticisms of educational research in the UK, western and eastern continental Europe and the USA, the following article summarises the findings of a study based on the analysis of some of the most influential texts that criticised educational research in the UK.

Oancea, A. (2005) 'Criticisms of educational research: key topics and levels of analysis', *British Educational Research Journal*, 31 (2): 157–83.

The following interesting paper considers the idea of a crisis in educational research. Some conventional expressions of that 'crisis' are examined in terms of their assumptions about what is 'proper' to educational research.

Peim, N. (2009) 'Thinking resources for educational research methods and methodology', *International Journal of Research and Method in Education*, 32 (3): 235–48.

Is ethical regulation a good thing? The article below questions whether ethics committees are capable of making sound judgments about the ethics of what is proposed and practised in particular research projects. In addition, the legitimacy of such regulation is questioned, on ethical grounds. Finally, it is argued that increased regulation will not raise the 'ethical standard' of social science and will probably worsen the quality of what it produces. It is a useful article for those wishing to adopt a critical position to concepts and source materials.

Hammersley, M. (2009) 'Against the ethicists: on the evils of ethical regulation', *International Journal of Social Research Methodology*, 12 (3): 211–25.

Finally, below is a text which presents a journey into the theory of qualitative research, as represented in this book. See in particular, Chapter 1, 'Introduction to The Discipline and Practice of Qualitative Research'.

Denzin, N.K. and Lincoln, Y. (eds) (2003) *The Landscape of Qualitative Research: Theories and Issues*, 2nd edn. London: Sage.

Section 2

Carrying out Research

3

Ethnographic practitioner research

Victoria Cooper with Carole Ellis

Chapter overview

Ethnographic research has become a method of choice for many practitioner researchers and has attained increased status in response to a series of initiatives which have targeted it as a vehicle to enhance professional practice (the Common Core of Skills and Knowledge: CWDC, 2010; the Early Years Foundation Stage: DCSF, 2008a). Ethnographic researchers have been strident in their reflective accounts of the benefits of using both ethnographic instruments and critical reflection as a means to capture rich educational experience (Clark and Moss, 2001; Tricoglus, 2001). Few accounts of practitioner experiences of designing and conducting research have surfaced. Who better to describe the coal-face experience of doing ethnographic practitioner research than the practitioners themselves? This chapter attempts to address this issue and utilises the recent student experience of a family support worker, Carole, who completed a small-scale ethnographic study as part of her Foundation Degree in Early Years, to illustrate the key features of this approach.

I have organised this chapter to introduce the reader to practitioner research and what this can mean within the context of education.

Using the practitioner research example provided by Carole, I go on to examine the key strands within the research process, particularly the importance of representing lived experience and critical reflection. I also examine the shifting relationship between the 'researcher' and the 'research participants' in response to the increase in collaborative approaches to enhance participant perspectives. I draw almost exclusively upon the application of participant research methods to explore practitioner investigation as a form of strategic research.

What is practitioner research?

The potential within practitioner research to challenge, promote change and increase knowledge is well documented (for example, Appleby, 2010; Tricoglus, 2001).

> Practitioner research offers the practitioner the opportunity to see the familiar in new and very different ways and this can be a powerful mechanism for changing and developing knowledge and practice in a particular setting. (Tricoglus, 2001: 137)

The underlying assumption here is that research can serve two distinct yet interactive purposes: development of the person (practitioner professional development) and development of the profession (innovation and change). Critical reflective analysis lies at the heart of both processes and is a key focus for this discussion.

Tricoglus (2001) draws attention to the complexity of practitioner research which does not have a defined approach, set of clearly defined principles or techniques. In many respects this reflects the nature of professional practice and research which are both flexible and fit for purpose. Researchers select approaches and instruments for gathering data based on the focus, audience and objective. Similarly, practitioners adopt different styles according to the needs of the profession. The emphasis upon audience and need are important here and begs the question, who is the research for?

Practitioner research has a varied audience. This may include children, parents, youths, the practitioner, the profession as a whole and placement setting, society and so forth. An important feature of all research is the notion that it speaks to and relates to its audience; it has both credibility and relevance. This is a dense area and one which has been widely debated in relation to how research reflects real experience, is representative, reliable and valid (Denscombe, 2010).

By its very definition practitioner research refers to the gathering of data by practitioners, within case study/placement settings with a view to developing greater knowledge and understanding. The idea is that by critically analysing practice, practitioners can action change, solve problems and so develop their practice based on greater insight and knowledge (Tricoglus, 2001). In this respect it is strategic. For many, this is a breath of fresh air within an environment which has been heavily burdened by top-down policy-driven initiatives. It also presents a shift in thinking, as research *by* practitioners *for* practitioners denotes increased credibility and relevance.

Educational research has witnessed a broadening of methodologies and approaches, from a traditional dependence on quantitative claims for objectivity to more interpretive, qualitative methods (Janzen, 2008). The underlying foundation for this approach rests upon the belief that the objective measurement of educational experience is neither possible nor valuable (Eisner, 1993). Conventional assumptions have become 'problematized', including notions of truth and certainty (Janzen, 2008: 288). In contrast to quantitative studies which aim to measure and quantify experience, ethnographic approaches are centrally focused on developing greater insight and depth of understanding.

A wealth of creative research approaches have been developed and utilised to embrace the commitment to capturing rich and real experience. Einarsdottir (2005) used disposable and digital cameras with young children as a means of expression as did Stephenson (2009) in the exploration of children's interests within an early years setting. Dockett and Perry (2005) examined children's experiences of school through their drawings and accompanying written narratives. Clark and Moss (2001) used a mixture of ethnographic instruments to collate children's experiences from a number of perspectives, including photographs, map-making, conferencing and participant observation. In each case the aims are pretty much the same, as a tool to capture experience from the participant perspective. As Lincoln (2010) describes it, research of this kind seeks to explore the many layers, levels and ingredients in social life, which are woven together to present a thick experience. So how can a practitioner researcher set about capturing personal experience?

The section which follows introduces practitioner research, drawing upon Carole's work, with a view to providing the reader with a sense of what this type of research can mean within the context of education.

The focus of practitioner research: representing lived experience

Here (Ellis, 2007 unpublished: 13), Carole introduces us to the focus of her research which aimed to explore the needs and interests of fathers with a view to enhancing father participation within an early years setting.

> I want to find out what fathers want not what the government are wanting of fathers ... I am seeking insight, not statistical perceptions ...

Carole's objective encapsulates the historical debate in educational research which questions how best to understand lived experience (Hammersley, 1993) as she stresses the importance of fathers articulating their own needs and views. The emphasis upon seeking insight is potentially empowering for both practitioner researchers and research participants and has evolved from developments within the field of ethnographic research.

While Carole set out with a very open intention to see how she could 'enhance paternal engagement at a Fathers Group at the Children's Centre', her research approach was strategic and flexible to suit the needs and issues within her work-based setting, as she describes:

> My research will influence my decision as to whether I should initiate such a group and provide the evidence needed to put together a project plan which is a process I must perform before any new sessions can be implemented at the children's centre. (Ellis, 2007 unpublished: 1)

Spradley (1979) describes the different approaches that ethnographic research can take, including the development of knowledge and understanding, advancement of a specific theory, or more strategic approaches to respond to problems or issues within a given context. Carole's research had a wide focus set against a backdrop of literature which recognised the need for professionals to support families (*Every Child Matters*, DfES, 2004) and promote father participation and engagement where possible (*Children's Plan*, DCSF, 2007; *Aiming High for Children: Supporting Families*, DfES 2007a) at the time, significantly driving development of local provision. Fathers are a hard to reach group, as Carole acknowledges upon reflection of her own experience and workplace setting where father engagement is low:

> Our services offer early education integrated with child care, family support and outreach to parents and children and we should be engaging with fathers who previously have been excluded from services and whose children are at risk of poor outcomes and all these facts have to be closely monitored to see just how far different groups of fathers have accessed services and gain feedback regarding what they thought of them. (Ellis, 2007 unpublished: 5)

A key question then was how she could reach such a group and gather evidence which would allow her to consider the feasibility of establishing a fathers group or not. As Carole suggests:

> In order to help me decide which methods of data collection would be most useful in this study I decided to think about what I needed to find out. After much reflection I decided it might be difficult to observe effectively because at the time I had little contact with fathers. I had to consider the practicalities of how much time I had to undertake research and what methods of accumulating evidence from fathers was most appropriate. (Ellis, 2007 unpublished: 10)

Here we can see how Carole contemplates her research approach and methods in the light of what she wishes to find out. This takes account of how practitioner research methods are very much driven by research questions that need to be asked and not the other way around. The focus of her practitioner research was open and revolved around a specific issue and how she, as a practitioner, could address this strategically, by increasing her knowledge and appreciation of the area, for example:

> I consulted current service users at the Children's Centre and I found there was a fathers group already well established and run by the Baptist Church ... I recognised that in order to start collecting information I would need to build relationships with the fathers in the hope that they would provide information for my research. I would need to attend several sessions if I was to effectively achieve this ...

Here (Ellis, 2007 unpublished: 12), Carole recognises the importance of accessing fathers groups to gain insight into their experiences. Experience is by its very nature subjective, multi-faceted and difficult to actually pin down. Attempts to access and understand such diverse experience have drawn upon ethnographic approaches which have positioned the researcher as observer, participant and co-constructor of lived experience (Clark and Moss, 2001; Powell et al., 2006). Willis (2004) stresses how behaviour cannot be explained from the confines of a library. Those seeking genuine understanding of lived experience must go into the field and discover how different people make sense of their own lives. This neatly summarises the very essence of ethnographic research: as a necessity for understanding lived social experience. As an approach it is naturalistic and invites the researcher to become part of what they seek to understand. In this way the researcher acknowledges and also reflects upon their potential impact upon the research process.

While Carole did not undertake the full participant observation characteristic of ethnographic research, she did utilise ethnographic data collection instruments, including field observation, to gather the views and experiences of fathers. So in contrast to quantitative research methods which set out to test a theory or measure behaviour following manipulation by the researcher, Carole adopted a practitioner ethnographic approach in which her role was very much guided by the needs of the research and her participants. The position of the researcher is important here and it is necessary to examine how this role has changed in response to shifting perceptions of agency and collaboration within the research process.

Repositioning the researcher role

Carole wanted to enhance paternal involvement within her own placement setting and rather than just go out and establish a fathers' group, she wanted firstly to see if this was welcomed by the local community and so worth developing. In this way Carole designed her research to:

> Foster attitudes and values that build positive relationships based on trust. I found I frequently needed to be flexible, sensitive and aware of social and political contexts ... Build relationships with fathers in the hope that they would provide information for my research. (Adapted from Ellis, 2007 unpublished)

Carole stresses how 'they' would provide the information and here we can see the change in emphasis from her, the researcher as expert, to the importance of her participants in being active agents within the research process. This demonstrates how ethnographic researchers develop greater insight and understanding and have repositioned the relationship between the 'researcher' and the 'researched'. Rather than presenting the participant, be it a child, youth or adult as an object of research, ethnographic research positions them as collaborator (Wohlwend, 2009). This reflects developments within the sociology of education and increasing emphasis placed upon children, as well as youths and adults, as being active constructors of their own experiences (Powell et al., 2006). Research participants are considered 'valuable experts' in their cultures (Janzen, 2008) and partners in the research dynamic (Christensen and Prout, 2005). Acknowledging the co-construction of meaning within education has provided a 'voice' to young children, youths and marginalised groups previously silenced within education. This further denotes a transformation in approaches which now use a variety of instruments to both capture and represent experience.

In order to develop key relationships with the local fathers, Carole had to penetrate fathers' groups where she could engage with fathers in order to access their views and experiences. Carole designed a practitioner research approach that would allow her to visit fathers' groups, observe and talk to fathers informally, and so gain some insight into their views and experiences, for example:

> My initial investigations were to monitor the engagement and quality that the group offered. I wanted to observe and question just what it is that the church offers that attracts fathers' interest … My aim when accessing the group was to remain honest and open and discuss with the fathers their thoughts, opinions and ideas. (Ellis, 2007 unpublished: 12)

The role of the practitioner researcher then is somewhat different to what may be regarded as a traditional research role. They neither impose upon nor manipulate their data collection, but instead facilitate an approach in which the participants are free to share their experiences as they see fit. In this way ethnographic research is grounded. This can be a difficult concept to grasp as it runs counter to the many connotations within traditional research which emphasise the need to control data for the sake of researcher reliability. The practitioner researcher has quite a challenge, not only to capture lived experience but to represent the reality of this experience from the participants' perspective and not their own. So how can this be achieved? The focus on meaning and voicing of experience are important here. To develop a rich understanding of experience necessitates that participants give meaning to their own lives, as they see it, and use their own voices, or any other means of representation, to tell their own story (Cooper, 2010).

Carole carefully considered not only how to access fathers by observing and participating in local fathers groups, but also how fathers experiences are not isolated but develop within a 'wider socio-political and cultural context' in which families and communities are important, suggesting:

> There are significant social and political driving forces, which are influencing a response to meeting the needs of fathers. (Ellis, 2007 unpublished: 20)

In this reflection, adapted from her literature review, Carole acknowledges the context of father experience which is important but also a potential barrier to their participation. This was an important consideration as Carole had to develop an approach which acknowledged these important variables.

Carole integrated her own professional knowledge and experience working in the local community with other multi-agency professionals to establish key contacts with local ante-natal groups where fathers were present and church-led fathers groups. Carole was also careful in designing her research so she could access fathers, as a marginalised group, through mothers whom she had regular contact with. So as well as developing a methodology which utilised informal observations, field notes and conversations, Carole devised a questionnaire to address key issues for fathers which she could distribute via their partners. In this way she developed a multi-method research approach. She incorporates the work of Denscombe (2010) to examine the importance of contrasting perspectives and indicates how:

> Different methods mean the researcher can compare and contrast findings ... and that the more data collected on the same topic the richer the quality will be. (Ellis, 2007 unpublished: 11)

The application of a multi-method approach is characteristic of practitioner ethnography that utilises ethnographic instruments to increase the validity of data, researcher reliability and data triangulation. Data triangulation allows the researcher to explore a given area from a number of different perspectives, using a range of contrasting instruments to examine multiple views, inconsistencies as well as consistencies and so draw up a picture of practice which reflects the complexity of human lived experience.

This approach shares much with developments by Clark and Moss (2001) who established a multi-method mosaic approach to capture young children's experiences of their early years setting and to see how they could represent those experiences through a range of media. They utilised a number of complementary ethnographic instruments for data collection, including participant observation, child conferencing (a form of interviewing) and participatory methods such as map-making, tours and photograph-taking to develop a mixed approach in which both the researcher and the child were active partners in the research process. The child conferences and observations were designed to capture formal and informal data about the children's experiences in the early years setting. The participatory methods were applied to provide the children with an opportunity to represent their experiences, as a form of map-making, and take the lead. The children were asked to take the researcher on a tour of their environment. The children gave a running commentary on where they went on their tour, supplemented by photographs of key areas within the setting. Both the maps and photographs were used by the researcher as points for discussion. Clark and Moss (2001) describe the value of mosaic approaches for both practitioners and participants. Not only does it engage the participant and offer empowerment in areas which matter to them, but it potentially challenges practitioners on commonly held beliefs and values and so encourages depth of critical reflection.

Practitioners are in an enviable position for conducting research of this kind. Not only do they have access and well established relationships within an educational context, but they have what Glaser and Strauss (1967) define as 'theoretical sensitivity'. This refers to the knowledge and understanding of a given area which provides a clear background to research. This allows the practitioner researcher to integrate the knowledge that they already have about their setting, the children and aspects of the community to forge a backdrop to their exploration. Carole discusses her own professional practice knowledge which was useful in following up the many community links she had established with other professionals as a means to access fathers groups, and also in equipping her with the *sensitivity* and *appreciation* to know what questions to ask and how to find out more. This led Carole to build upon her considerable background as a practitioner and explore issues about father engagement through extensive reading, liaison with other professionals and attendance at conferences where social justice issues for fathers were highlighted as important.

> I do have some knowledge but my aim is to raise paternal engagement and I need to find out what are the barriers or problems that stop fathers from engaging in services we currently offer ... Information can now be seen on the Internet and has provided me with valuable insight into the whole issue of 'Fathers' Rights' and the driving forward of fathers' agendas ... (Adapted from Ellis, unpublished 2007)

This is a central feature of practitioner research as it builds in the professional knowledge and background experience of the practitioner as a springboard for further analysis. Research of this kind, however, is vulnerable to researcher interpretation. Utilising professional and practitioner knowledge runs the danger of being guided by personal beliefs, values and assumptions which may restrict research progress. Carole was mindful of this, as she acknowledges in her own critical reflections:

> I hope that my views, values and initial assumptions will not impose on my research, it is my intention to reflect continually on my thoughts, findings and bias so that I can reach a true understanding of the outcomes and at all times give attention to ethical considerations. I wanted to gather information that will assist me to solve theoretical and practical problems and aid me to implement evidence-based practice. (Ellis, 2007 unpublished: 1)

The strength and credibility of research which is culturally and socially contextualised, case-specific and vulnerable to researcher interpretation and bias are issues which have been extensively debated (Hammersley, 1993; Tangen, 2008) and are considered potential threats to the validity of ethnographic practitioner research. Tangen (2008) draws upon the work of Fay (1996) to examine the paradoxical nature of insider knowledge, which can be viewed as an advantage for being sensitive to certain themes, while conversely being a potential hindrance. Schiller and Einarsdottir (2009) advocate in-depth researcher questioning and reflection as a means to scrutinise the methods adopted and the impact of the researcher upon and within the research process.

While ethnographic research does not make any claims for scientific objectivity, the importance of research rigour cannot be ignored. The limitations of subjective interpretations are not a threat exclusive to ethnographic research, but as Lincoln warns:

> Claims are suspect and provisional, at best, and there is no single method which is guaranteed to produce final truth. (2010: 4)

So interpretation by any researcher runs the risk of misunderstanding and misrepresentation. Critical reflection lies at the heart of practitioner research as an instrument to challenge assumptions and beliefs which may interfere with the research process and data collection and also as a means to question, interrogate and deepen knowledge and understanding.

The reflective process

The importance of reflection, as articulated here by Carole (Ellis, 2007 unpublished: 26), is widely acknowledged (Appleby, 2010; Bolton, 2005;

Stephenson, 2009) and at the time of writing is a feature of statutory guidelines which recognise it as a medium for continuing professional development (Common Core of Skills and Knowledge: CWDC, 2010; Early Years Foundation Stage: DCSF, 2008a) and as a means to inject rigour into research practice (Schiller and Einarsdottir, 2009).

> By scrutinizing my personal beliefs, my knowledge and about gender issues, the socio-political arena, cultural norms, working hours, and allowing time for 'tuning in' are all issues that I have explored and I recognize create barriers to paternal engagement.

Appleby (2010) examines the wealth of terms that have been used to describe what reflection can mean: defining it as critical, a social practice and an art. She extends this further to explore the different types of reflection that can be employed, from reflective learning and writing to critical reflection and reflective action. While each of these themes are important, this discussion is more concerned with how reflection is experienced from a practitioner research perspective, with particular emphasis upon research rigour, critical reflective analysis and purposefulness.

Carole presents a very personal account of her learning and development. Her analogy of 'tuning in' is an interesting one which focuses on how taking the time to conduct research and scrutinise her practice demonstrated how she was prepared to be challenged, to be critical of herself and others. Bolton (2005) emphasises the importance of being critical so avoiding the reduction of reflection to a mere 'naval gazing' exercise (cited in Appleby, 2010: 20). Clearly there is very little point in reflecting upon something which you have no desire to change or feel doesn't warrant development. Likewise, there is little value in reflecting upon something without a critical eye which invites you to explore alternatives. The critical edge to reflection invites the practitioner to consider differing perspectives and invite personal development and change where necessary, as Carole describes:

> Research has developed informed confidence, enhanced my early year's professional knowledge and understanding and made me examine and reflect on my personal practice and my personal views. It has involved looking at change that will improve the quality of the services I offer to the families I support. (Adapted from Ellis, 2007 unpublished)

Carole adopted a critical reflective approach which allowed her to consider other perspectives which were important to her analysis – and not just her own, as she suggests:

> Attendance at a father's direct conference gave me many issues to consider and reflect on, the first and foremost was to address my personal view of paternal engagement and would my views prohibit me from actively encouraging fathers to engage in sessions that we run from the centre ... The research has contributed to a greater understanding of a father's engagement from a male perspective ... Attendance at fathers' groups gave me insight into issues men face. (Ellis, 2007 unpublished: 8)

Through acknowledging different perspectives, Carole was able to consider how fathers feel in relation to their participation and engagement and attempt to set aside her own beliefs and values which could potentially impact upon her findings. By accessing different fathers groups and gaining some insight into how fathers feel in relation to engagement and participation, Carole perceived things from a different angle. At times this was uncomfortable. This was particularly evident when she describes a critical incident when joining a local fathers group:

> Being in this male environment was sometimes uncomfortable. I heard a comment that was directed at me deliberately by one respondent who said, 'we don't have mums here, it's for dads only'. I found that this made me empathise with fathers who access services that we provide that are predominately female environments and how acceptance into a group is important to feeling valued and welcome. (Ellis, 2007 unpublished: 14)

Carole further describes how this incident encouraged her to reflect upon her role as a mother as well as her professional position, in which she became 'shocked that I did not allow my husband opportunities to tune into our children when they were little' (Ellis, 2007 unpublished: 22), so demonstrating the power of critical reflection on a personal and professional level.

Critical reflection can often incite different perspectives to unfold counter-arguments and can challenge assumed practice and automatic ways of doing things. As a feature of research, critical reflection aligns itself to data triangulation in which it encourages the researcher to explore other perspectives which perhaps were not the initial focus of the research or even an area under investigation. Stephenson (2009) similarly describes this process as 'stepping back' from her research as a means to access authentic data. Stephenson's (2009) research had been designed to elicit young children's perspectives of their education centre environment and key interests using photographs (taken by her and the children) as points for discussion. In taking time and 'stepping back' from her research focus she discovered that one particular young boy could not represent his interest through the photographs taken – but that following discussion with him and getting to know him she unveiled his personal interest which stepped outside the remit of her study. This represented an important learning incident for Stephenson and further highlights a key message for researchers and practitioners seeking to develop greater understanding of key issues in education. Taking a critical stance is clearly very important as researchers attempt to resist being restricted by their own data collection instruments and open to what their participants have on offer or wish to share.

The value of critical reflection as a research tool to examine different perspectives is evident as this enables the practitioner researcher to unveil rich data which in turn reflects the inconsistencies of real life. It is important also to consider how data and reflections of this kind can be used and what their purposes are. So, even though the benefits of critical reflection – as a means to gather data from a range of perspectives – is useful, its value lies in how this data can be used.

The very essence and purpose of research is neatly illustrated here, as Carole demonstrates the importance that all research feeds into something; be it practice, policy, theory or knowledge, its value lies in how things can be improved:

> This process has taken several months, but has provided the time to reflect effectively and allows me to apply what I have learnt to fathers, children and the wider community. Introducing the 'fathers group' will allow me to develop, demonstrate and improve my practice. (Ellis, 2007 unpublished: 26)

This presents a very active position in which Carole can clearly articulate her role as a professional:

> I have become far more familiar with policy, which gives me a better understanding about what I do, why I do it and how I apply what I have learnt to inform future practice. (Ellis, 2007 unpublished: 23)

As well as providing an opportunity to reflect on where things need to be changed and developed, Carole demonstrates the capacity for critical reflection to inform future practice:

> I am in a position to enhance paternal engagement through support, outreach work and attending such a group. I need to become acquainted with the fathers and find out what other opportunities they would like access to, e.g. classes about child development, first aid, career choices, budgeting … We need to think about making the setting father friendly, inclusive, innovative and welcoming. Through consultation I acknowledge that fathers can shape the services we offer. (Ellis, 2007 unpublished: 22)

Carole reflects upon how she will disseminate her research to other colleagues and the wider community:

> I have accumulated a lot of evidence that has aided my understanding and I have developed my professional and leadership skills by producing an information pack that I will make available to colleagues at the children's centre. (Ellis, 2007 unpublished: 26)

Having the confidence to *share* and disseminate research findings and learning represents a huge development and is discussed in Chapter 7. Not only does it recognise the value of local knowledge and practitioner experience but presents an environment through which sharing and community learning is valued. This view shares much with Wenger's (1998) work on the value of communities of practice in facilitating a medium for shared meaning and collaboration. The desire to change and develop practice based upon collaborative reflection and new meaning-making here is central. Edwards (2004) examines the difficult relationship between research and practice and highlights the importance of collaboration between participants and researchers as a means to provide effective dissemination and sharing of research findings.

For me, Carole's reflective account offers an insight into her journey as a practitioner researcher. But more than this, it evokes something of the commitment necessary for practitioner researchers to undertake in-depth analysis of this kind and the importance of preparation: being prepared to be critical of oneself and others, being prepared to develop practice and – finally – being prepared to change both personally and professionally.

Summary

Practitioner research has evolved from developments in educational research which have utilised ethnographic instruments as a means to gain knowledge and understanding of educational issues. Gaining greater insight presents opportunities for strategic change and development. This can have a profound impact upon professional development, for the individual practitioner and for the profession more widely. As a central feature of practitioner research, critical reflective analysis provides opportunities for practitioners to critically evaluate their practice, challenge taken-for-granted beliefs and assumptions and so instigate change and development where necessary. This chapter has drawn upon the work of one work-based learning student to illustrate the development of practitioner research, its many strengths, features and characteristics, with a view to providing other researchers and practitioner researchers some insight into how this approach can be applied.

I am very grateful to Carole for allowing me some insight into her experiences of practitioner research, the difficulties she has faced and the valuable lessons she has learnt along the way. By stepping into Carole's world, albeit briefly, I have gained both knowledge and greater understanding of what it takes to research in practice. This has further provided me with an opportunity to reflect upon my own position as an ethnographic researcher and appreciate the value of what research of this kind can offer.

Further reading

For useful further reading on the broader topic of provision for children and families see:

Early Childhood Research and Practice (*ECRP*), a peer-reviewed electronic journal sponsored by the Early Childhood and Parenting (ECAP) Collaborative at the University of Illinois at Urbana-Champaign, covering topics related to the development, care and education of children from birth to approximately age 8 (online at: http://ecrp.uiuc. edu/). *ECRP* emphasises articles reporting on practice-related research and development, and on issues related to practice, parent participation and policy.

To inform a critical understanding about the use of case studies in research practice, the following well researched article concludes that case study is essentially a convenient label that can be applied to just about any social research project, especially perhaps when no other term seems available. It considers what might be done instead.

Tight, M. (2010) 'The curious case of case study: a viewpoint,' *International Journal of Social Research Methodology*, 13 (4): 329–39.

Finding a theoretical position: using 'literature' to support investigation and practice

Jude Simms with Sue Callan

Chapter overview

The qualities required for effective work with children and families include the ability to relate and apply 'theory' to practice. This chapter is based on a reflective discussion concerning the way in which use of 'expert opinion' underpins our work in developing, managing and leading provision. It demonstrates how source material is accessed for use in supporting children, families and colleagues in both formal and informal practice investigations and, as such, illustrates the process of professional enquiry. Our reflection considers the symbiotic relationship between the different models of research encountered by experienced practitioners as they seek to meet standards for academic and qualification requirements while, at the same time, addressing the improvement of provision through reflective practice in the quality cycle. As such, the chapter offers an example to dissertation students of the significance of 'literature review' to research. At the same time, it will remind practitioner researchers that reading 'expert opinion' (i.e. literature) is itself a way of collecting 'data' for work-based projects and offers some strategies for doing so. Definition of 'literature' in the context of work-based investigation will emerge through the various practical examples provided. Throughout, the focus remains on the significance of sector-related literature to leadership and management, where work-based investigation forms the cornerstone for effective provision and community development. As a result, we have included as quotation direct contributions from the discussion on Jude's experience. Practitioners are often anxious that research removes them from the focus on children and families. We argue that, on the contrary, it facilitates and enables insightful contribution to communities of practice – an argument extended in the final chapter.

Context and rationale for engaging with literature

As an Early Years Professional (EYP) in England, Jude leads a team of eight part-time practitioners in a split-site committee-run playgroup drawing children from three counties. The staff team, who come through the parent base, have been with the group for between 3 and 15 years. Qualification levels range from 2 to 5 and two staff can be described as graduate leaders. Continuing professional development (CPD) activities are a requirement for all members of the team, as are annual appraisals. The children come from diverse backgrounds and a wide range of development and ability levels. In the parent body, levels of education run from PhD to those with significant literacy problems. The playgroup is a feeder group for eight primary schools.

The featured team is representative of the policy framework that emerged from Every Child Matters (DfES, 2004) and related legislation within the government administration from 1997–2010. There is evidence of professionalisation of the workforce, multi-agency working, participation in local children and family networks and ongoing commitment to CPD. It is worth emphasising the point that staff 'emerge' through their initial involvement with the group as parent members – representative of the ethos and culture of the traditional pre-school movement. The challenge for such staff is to develop their responses to children and their own practice from this 'intuitive' parent focus in order to represent the requirements of the Common Core of Skills and Knowledge (CCSK) (CWDC, 2010) or the EYP standards (CWDC, 2009). They must become aware that a landscape of practice is far wider than their own small setting and that personal 'knowledge' and attitudes should be 'informed' in terms of the early years tradition as well as statutory requirements. As such, CPD activities and 'research' in both vocational and higher education contexts extend the boundaries of existing personal 'knowledge'. Individual practitioners engage in a journey that will take them from exploration of practice inside the setting to investigation of the external drivers for their daily roles, responsibilities and inter-actions with children and families. This is the key purpose of 'litera-ture' search – practitioners will be seeking examples in practice and on practice in order to facilitate development of provision. They will also be finding explanations for the models and approaches adopted in wider professional contexts as part of reflecting on their own val-ues and perspectives, the focus of any research enquiry.

This is represented in Jude's experience. She notes:

> From very early on in my studies, when I began as a mum helper in the play-group and went back to college to gain my Diploma in Pre-School Practice (Level 3), I recognised the necessity to reflect on why and how I manage change. It has always been vital to me to protect the 'learning through play' ethos of the group. The course introduced the possibilities of engaging in research and a realisation that it was acceptable to critically debate theory in relation to current practice and vice versa. I found a voice and a medium through which I could channel critical and creative thinking. My first experi-ence of relating theory to practice in my (then) new role as manager was during one of the first pre-school Ofsted inspections. Being able to call on up-to-date information and having theory embedded practice, enabled me to defend our ethos and strategies for working.
>
> As my playgroup role has developed, being well read has helped focus and galvanise the direction the whole staff team has taken. Every early years prac-titioner will have had experience of this type of research. The barrage of changes faced by the sector over the last 15 years has been formidable from educational policy through to safeguarding practices. Practitioners at all levels have had to adapt and change their practice to incorporate legislative require-ments, the Common Core of Skills and Knowledge (CCSK) (CWDC, 2010), National Strategies (DCSF, 2008b) and Children's Plan (DCSF, 2007) to name but a few obvious examples. Personally, I enjoy a challenge and these changes have tested my innovation and creativity. As a manager, I recognise and have experienced that the resulting changes need to be carefully managed for chil-dren, families and particularly the staff. At the core of any setting and funda-mental to its ethos, survival and therefore success, is the team – they need respect, sensitive support and nurturing.

Two things of note here – engaging with reading and research is a prerequisite for personal professional development (discussed in Chapter 7). It is the means by which Jude acquired her professional 'voice' and underpins her ability to lead, manage and support col-leagues. This is consistent with the formal requirements of academic qualification and models of research discussed in the editors' intro-duction. On the other hand, knowledge of 'literature' (here encom-passing the full spectrum of practice frameworks) is a key leadership quality and is currently represented, in England, by the standards for EYP status (CWDC, 2009). The EYP is expected to develop and sustain a resource bank in order to inform the ability to support the Early Years Foundation Stage (EYFS) (DCSF, 2008a) and continued quality improvement for children's daily experience of settings. Jude talks about 'theory embedded practice' and offers the following example of how work with children is enhanced by use of literature.

The cheese biscuit change

> I had been worrying about the salt content of the snack biscuit we offered the children, partly as a result of some basic research delivered by a fellow student on my Foundation Degree course. Having read research on child obesity, I considered the snack we were providing, which at that time consisted of a sweet or cheese biscuit and milk or water, at a whole group snack time. My research on the internet turned up information about childhood obesity and the recommended salt levels. Simple healthy eating interventions, such as including fruit and raw vegetables as snacks, was promoted in several early years magazines. Also the idea of having 'free flow' or café-style snack, promoted by the Pre-School Learning Alliance had long been niggling away at the back of my consciousness. I had always felt that as many children did not sit to the table at home anymore and chat as a family, that playgroup needed to promote that side of the eating experience. I consider that introducing too many changes at once was not a good start. With any research project there is a need to be concise and I needed to focus in on the essence of what I was trying to achieve. I decided that the cheese biscuit item was my focus, but I also kept in the back of my mind the other items I wished to tackle and put them in order of priority. Just as one would do during a written piece of research, these items I hoped to introduce if and when the time was right.

This example shows how a seemingly small change action becomes an 'informal' work-based investigation. We see how Jude is aware of a social concern about health and accesses information to see if the playgroup can improve the nutrition of the snack provided. In fact, this piece contains a number of *assumptions* – about the salt content of the biscuits and children's domestic mealtimes in particular. Significantly, the engagement with literature and source investigation is a means by which assumptions and personal theories can be investigated and informed decision-making supported. Jude makes use of the Internet and professional journals as information sources. In so doing, Jude is developing her own knowledge of health issues and strategies for improving diet, and finding examples of effective practice in other settings. *At the same time* she is critically reflecting on aspects of provision that might be changed to give the children greater agency over this aspect of their experience in the setting – demonstrating reflexive practice. Her ideas are based on material promoted by a sector-recognised organisation and discussed in practitioner text books (Anning et al., 2009; Pugh and Duffy, 2006). What Jude describes here is a change spiral that develops as the team and the children become involved, representing the quality agenda as noted in the editors' introduction. The progress of the work-based investigation also makes use of research techniques discussed in Chapter 5.

> I began by sounding out different session staff. Some were interested and positive about change, some worried about limiting choice for the children and some were very resistant. The issue was then discussed at a staff meeting where everyone had a voice and ideas for possible changes were invited and recorded. I presented a summary of our discussion and my informal research evidence to the staff team. We decided to trial low salt crackers *or* sweet biscuit, and fruit (playgroup would provide apples and parents were invited to provide one piece of fruit or veg a week to supplement the choice). Within a month this was the accepted norm and the parents became interested in and contributed to what their child was choosing at snack by providing a variety of fruit and vegetables. This initial research then led to further investigation of whole group snack versus an open rolling snack available throughout morning session. Observations (collecting 'data') of the positive responses and in discussion with the children supported the changes. Different members of staff have researched different angles, looking at children's independence during snack, including pouring skills, self-regulation, availability of drinking water during session for self-care, self-esteem issues surrounding choice, communication that arises from small group snack versus large group snack. In this way, snack has developed from a simple provision of refreshment to an activity that can provide opportunities for the children to progress across every area of their development.
>
> If literature/research had not supported this project, the spiral of development of 'snack time' could not have happened. The change started five years ago and continues today. The most recent change is looking at how we site the snack area so the children can really have ownership of it. The thing that really shines out to me, as a leader manager, is that by enabling discussion and encouraging research and questioning of any initiative, the staff team and the children will 'own' the resulting changes and that change will therefore be sustained.

Literature and constructive change

Jude's conclusion is supported by Kemmis (2001). By gathering literature to support change, but also to demonstrate how that has to be valid and authentic, the whole team, all of different abilities and motivation, can contribute effectively to the process and therefore the resulting change is sustainable. The idea that research and practice can be brought together stem from the views of Freire (1973) who proposed that the teacher reflects on and engages in constructive change. The research process has provided a thorough and logical process to Jude's thinking and grounds the innovative idea in reality, thus providing a formal structure (methods) for creativity. The knowledge creation process in this sense is firmly grounded in experience with theorising connected to sense-making and action planning within the group, rather than imposed 'arbitrarily in a disconnected manner from outside' (Yelland et al., 2008: 17). In this construction of 'insider' investigation (outlined in Chapters 2 and 3) and the practical example of the cheese biscuit exchange, we can also see that 'informal' work-based research is ongoing. Because it facilitates reflection, it will be longitudinal and must necessarily contribute to continuous enhancement of practice and the children's experience. Engagement with literature provides validity and credibility to the outcomes, whether or not the material is 'published' – a point extended in Chapter 6.

Developing literature investigations – building up a resource bank

Jude's example demonstrates that practitioners are using literature 'intuitively' and the range of sources drawn on for daily practice is clearly apparent. Professional publications and academic journals as well as practitioner-focused publications are useful as a means by which teams can identify further reading. Practice documents (for example, the EYFS (DCSF, 2008a)) and publications released as guidance to support national strategies (for example, *Social and Emotional Aspects of Development*, (DCSF, 2008c)) usually include theoretical references and signpost further source materials. Be aware that all government publications will be based around prevailing policy interests, so you need to be open to investigating alternative perspectives in order to construct a critical approach. Sources such as these are practical resources at the heart of a work-based enquiry. In the next example, we examine a 'formal' project that necessitated a structured literature investigation. In this event, the literature search – of a wider range of materials – becomes a method of investigation in its own right and can offer a means of refining the construction and focus of a project to manageable proportions – usually a problem for student researchers and practitioners alike.

Engaging with 'discourse': moving towards more formal projects and investigations

We have seen that for 'informal' research in settings, the literature investigation is the means by which we can identify current and emerging practice developments in order to improve provision. Significantly, in a 'formal' project, this search is written up and reported as a 'review' of literature as part of published outcomes (discussed in Chapter 6). 'Formal' research at any level is also informed by such practice – for example extensive review of international literature informed the approach to, and development of, *Birth to Three Matters* (DfES, 2002) which proved so significant to the evolution of EYFS five years later. At this point it is worth clarifying the concept of 'discourse' used in this text as it applies to research dynamics. This term is used to describe the prevailing body of academic knowledge which forms the theoretical underpinning for practice in the sector. This is informed by 'big science' research as described by Safford and Hancock (2010) and will usually determine the accepted system of 'beliefs' and values held by and influencing social, cultural and policy frameworks which result in accepted principles for practice. Engaging with literature – the body of recognised 'expert' knowledge represented in this 'discourse' – enables the work-based investigator to access the various debates within it. The practitioner will engage in developing a personal theoretical position in relation to practice in settings as part of implementing the accepted 'discourse', but – we argue – will also generate the 'discourse' for their own provision through interrogating the sources explored from the wider context. What results is a local 'discourse', most readily recognised in the workplace as part of the ethos of the setting.

Academic and practice-based researchers alike share the benefits of source investigation, which:

- give you confidence to 'argue your corner';

- provide evidence from theory and practice to support change;

- offer that 'a-ha!' moment when you recognise how your thinking relates to early childhood 'discourse';

- bring thorough grounding to your ideas – academic literature backs up intuition and instinct but should also challenge your assumptions;

- refine your 'question' and methods as you distinguish what is to be researched;

- develop implementation of government initiatives in a personalised, sustainable way;

- ensure reflective thinking and support reflective practice;

- underpin, challenge and support quality early years practice and local/setting policies.

In the next section, Jude reviews her 'formal' investigation into the process of transition from playgroup to school.

Getting started

> Once the issue became apparent – 'how can we make the children's transition to school as smooth as possible?' – I began background reading alongside discussion with the team to try and get different perspectives and to isolate the facts of the matter. My method for approaching this was to be as open minded as possible and read everything and anything that I could find. I also engaged in discussion with anyone who would listen and networked with colleagues, which threw up little gems of information from unexpected sources. I tried to build up a mental picture of the issue surrounded by these pieces of information, which then began to interlink.

Where to look and what to consult

Check out what is already out there relating to your subject because you are unlikely to be unique. This engagement with the existing discourse makes sure your work is informed, valid and reliable. Novice researchers should beware of the reliability of information sources from the Internet – use recognised research sites or authenticated articles. It is important to distinguish between *information* sites and *academic* sites that contribute to what is known as 'knowledge exchange' through debates and shared enquiry.

Academic journals contain the latest publications and recent research. They are invaluable because of their contemporary focus, offer innovative research methods and so are highly pertinent to current and emerging questions and issues. Check the list on the back of each journal to focus further reading and try not to get distracted by unrelated but interesting reports. Looking at journal research will firmly ground the work in academic thinking. At some point in a 'formal' project, it is helpful to check out other dissertations and research reports. At a practical level, this provides reassurance that other people also find a particular topic interesting and indicates possible lines of enquiry and other insights. The reference lists from such sources are also a valuable starting point for identifying material.

Reading sometimes difficult academic writing helps push personal learning boundaries and reflection, or challenges a previously unrecognised bias. This is important because it is often through the 'difficult' text that interesting discoveries are made that will challenge assumptions. One area in Jude's transition research showed that struggling with diversity, far from lowering children's self-esteem and their ability to cope, actually increased their resilience (Ecclestone, 2005). This challenged preconceptions and offered rigour in a 'critical' approach to writing (see Chapter 6).

Managing material and recording references

Use a reflective journal, diary, notebook or whatever method suits, but try to keep 'discussion' going with yourself, involving your network with colleagues, issues and dilemmas, and other pieces of information from magazines, television and the Internet. When collecting information, ensure you log referenced material – so often an excellent piece of evidence can't be used because details of the full reference have not been recorded – as this is vital for formal reporting. You will need author/s/editor/s, date/s, page numbers, title, chapter title, place, publisher: if an internet source, URL and data accessed. If you are writing for 'publication', such as a dissertation, you need to follow the guidelines of your awarding institution. Referencing details are a means of authenticating your work and offering further research. Referencing techniques are also modelled through reading academic writing and source lists – in this way inexperienced writers become used to using academic conventions.

Getting direction and refining ideas

Being methodical and logical and making mind maps helps. Jude set about exploring 'transitions' first in her specific context then approached the concept more widely to include the UK, government policy, the European Union, human resource policy and changes in industry. This takes the concept as wide as possible to allow for that 'slow knowing' (Claxton, 1997) and creative process (Fullan, 2001) to engage.

Keep the child and the experience of your setting at the centre of your investigation. For example, to 'ground' the transition project, Jude looked at the child in context (how they exist between the setting and home) and so narrowed the thought process down to specific children and the issue of self-esteem. During this focusing process Jude was simultaneously looking at related theory and UNICEF reports (2007, online) on how self-esteem is linked to the ability to function and learn.

Sharon Smith shows in Chapter 6 that it is important to use this 'review' process when reporting on literature for formal projects. Think of yourself as a private detective, gathering evidence to present in court to 'prove' a position. Formal/academic studies require you to make a case for and against the changes proposed – this is generally an unwritten part of the 'informal' process in settings as teams debate work-based practice initiatives (for instance, with the snack-time change).

To ground thinking to a definite point, student investigators often like to find a really pertinent quote that defines their motivation and ethos. For example, Fabien and Dunlop's statement: 'Such is the significance of early transitions for young children that it is essential that parents, educators, policy makers and politicians pay close attention to the young children's experiences in order to provide well for them' (2002: 1). This encompassed the key points of Jude's formal research – young children's experiences, transitions, inter-agency working, the political agenda and professional responsibilities in the process.

Impact of literature review on investigation

In general terms it is possible to see in this process that researching literature is vital for developing a thorough understanding of exactly *what* is being researched. Active practitioners all have good practical and intuitive understanding of what actually goes on and why. Reflective practitioners will also recognise that there are always other ways of doing something. Literature investigation gives supporting factual data and knowledge that can be utilised not only to make authentic change but that can be presented as evidence to regulatory bodies. This has proved essential in Jude's setting, where the team's local discourse is deeply rooted in shared practice, continually reflected upon and challenged. Government initiatives, unless a legal requirement, are not always suitable for every group of children. Changing with political whims can be detrimental to the setting, unless introduced and supported effectively. Each setting therefore needs to examine national initiatives by reflecting on the local context. Taking account of related literature can aid this process and enable the setting to either stay with their own systems, propose an alternative or adapt the initiative, resulting in a differentiated approach incorporating the new ideas as shown in the evolution of Linda Picken's work (2007 unpublished) discussed in Chapter 1.

Reading as a research method enables practitioners to make systematic, authentic and sustainable change based on theory and practice that supports individuals and the setting to deliver EYFS (DCSF, 2008a) and to meet CCSK requirements (CWDC, 2010). It fits well with the action planning, focus improvement plans, policies and self-evaluation forms (SEFs) that settings produce. Fundamentally, it is a feature of personal professionalism.

Jude's literature search resulted in a refined 'formal' project, which looked at improving children's experiences of transition. This helped keep the project focused, manageable and pertinent to the children and setting, but the interrogation of literature provided evidence from as wide a scope as possible. Keeping the project small and specific is also vital as it makes it manageable for a novice academic researcher. In reality, it is the relatively small changes from within an authentic team of early years practitioners that make a real difference to the children. Without the literature review, the issues of cheese biscuits and transitions may well have been resolved adequately but it is possible that the opportunity for further cycles of improvement and sustainable practical action would have been missed. We continue by acknowledging the impact on practice of this form of enquiry and the improvements in the experience of the children.

Impact of reading on professional practice and personal change

The literature review in the 'formal' transitions project helped Jude and her colleagues develop a format for inter-agency working, enabling 'joined up provision' as defined in legislation (DfES, 2006b). It provided evidence and practical examples of successful working with parents, teachers and head teachers. The research helped demonstrate to the reception teacher, head teacher and governors that the proposed transition recommendations were specific but also underpinned by the sector discourse which supported the school and its SEF, and was aligned with school culture. This project is still evolving and developing and the feedback from the families, reception class colleagues is very positive.

However, we also propose that the experience of 'informal' research (exemplified by the cheese biscuit exchange) provides practice-based investigators with skills and resources that will underpin their ability to meet 'formal' academic requirements. It could be argued that one is not superior to the other but will exist in a symbiotic relationship as the impact of workforce changes and qualification routes take effect.

Reading and networking are essential to the role of a leader. These activities provide grounding for ideas, theories and triangulation that validates actions and theory in practice. Both facilitate involvement in professional networks and the landscape of practice described in Chapter 7. After all, reflecting on/in/for practice as distinguished by Appleby (2010) creates 'new' approaches that are current and change that is sustainable. In order to be an effective 'agent of change' a practitioner needs to assess the quality of provision continually, to acknowledge what is done well and to seek strategies for improvement. Utilising colleagues as well as literature can provide another lens through which to view one's own performance. The concept of reflective lenses is constructed by Brookfield (1995) and has been recently outlined by Canning and Callan (2010) and Cooper (2010) in a discussion of work-based qualifications based on reflective practice. Having theoretical support can aid constructive discussion and enable challenges to established practice to be objective and purposeful. Just as practice needs supporting with theory, McNiff and Whitehead (2002) show that theory needs to be rooted in practice in order to be real.

Jude shows how her reflection is ongoing as the result of the transitions project:

While gathering research on 'transition ' it became evident to me that the issues involved in the transition process for children could be transposed to any group of people undergoing change including to my own personal journey. I recognise that each cycle of research has many facets and that the resulting change processes can be harnessed on personal, professional and political levels.

Literature for working with children and families

In work-based investigations, the researcher/practitioner does not always work as a detached 'other'. In this final section, we explore further the 'informal' research experienced by established practitioners. To do so, we have reflected on an example where a parent and colleagues have influenced local discourse because of the commitment to investigate and respond to a child's needs. This case study example has been selected to show that children's 'voices' can still drive practice, despite formalised requirements for practice and academic processes.

 Case study

A child came to the setting who was clearly able in terms of literacy markers, yet struggled to relate to her peers, displaying frustration through negative physical behaviour. The ensuing records made with the parents on shared pre-school experiences, family views and expectations were later discussed as a team. Some felt this child's individual play plan should focus on aspects of social and emotional development (SAED), while others felt it essential to look at potential 'gifted and talented' monitoring.

Collecting of information including networking, inter-agency work, *research and reading* was conducted as a team. Detailed observations were made, with the child's parents regularly consulted. The dilemma was eventually 'solved' by the child during a display of frustration – when asked to 'use words' (instead of actions), she replied in anguished tones 'but I don't have any words!' This immediately highlighted the need to equip her with emotional literacy words so that she could express herself effectively. The importance of an SAED focus while recognising the child's obvious abilities and the necessity to support the whole family in order for the child to progress securely and holistically was clarified. A Special Educational Needs Individual Education Plan (action) was drawn up in consultation with the child's parents and a copy was shared with another setting she attended. The family also borrowed a book on personal and emotional development (Dowling, 2003) from the setting 'library'.

This case study illustrates how a dedicated team 'owns' the commitment to continuous reflection and improvement. This is vital if the profile of the early years sector is to be raised. As a result of their research, Sylva et al. (2004) proposed the need for a graduate-level practitioner in pre-schools as a means of raising standards. This drive to professionalism highlights the necessity for theoretically embedded leadership and management which is informed, not merely espoused. 'Graduateness' has at its heart the engagement with 'research' and theory in practice that facilitates reflection and participation in a changing landscape of practice.

Summary

The chapter shows how reviewing literature provides factual evidence, practical policy-related advice, procedures and support for professional development. The process is itself representative of data gathering in terms of research processes, with clear examples of the nature of 'literature' in both 'formal' and 'informal' contexts. The use of source material helps practitioners explore and explain to interested parties the theoretical relevance of drivers for change – be they internal or external to the setting – providing a framework through which teams can explore their own values and approaches.

For Jude's team, one impact of the investigations outlined here has been detailed addendums for related setting policies, each representing continuous improvement in practice and making clear the relationship between work-based practice, research and quality of provision.

We have shown that social change begins in people's minds as they make choices about which values to espouse and how to live in the direction of those values (McNiff and Whitehead, 2002: 11). Research, as noted in Chapter 2, is an important part of this process of personal and professional development in the sector. In order to make change spiral progressively and be sustainable we need to think strategically and engaging with literature underpins this. It provides space to reflect individually and as a team, and enables the process of allowing theory and what is actually happening in practice to come together, allowing ideas for possible directions to develop. Overall, we hope to have supported the notion that the experience of 'research' – however defined – is the means by which practitioners develop a professional identity and voice informed by the philosophical and theoretical traditions of the sector.

Further reading

The purpose of the following article is to help make the research reading experience more manageable. It breaks the typical research manuscript down into several parts and offers a brief description of the purpose of each, as well as some tips for developing more clear interpretations and understandings.

Baum, A. and McMurray-Schwarz, P. (2007) 'Research 101: tools for reading and interpreting early childhood research', *Early Childhood Education Journal*, 34 (6), online at: http://www.springerlink.com/index/6322520228624476.pdf.

The following guide characterises practice-related research for the general reader and research student.

Candy, L. (2006) *Practice Based Research: A Guide*, CCS Report: 2006-V1.0 November. Sydney: Creativity & Cognition Studios, University of Technology. Online at: http://www.creativityandcognition.com/resources/PBR%20Guide-1.1-2006.pdf.

5

Activities to reflect your position as a researcher: creative approaches to research methods

Sue Callan with Tracy Davies, Carole Ellis and Alison Jackson

---

Chapter overview

The aim of this chapter is to promote practitioner confidence in adopting creative approaches to investigation. It considers the selection of activities for investigation as part of a continuing process of reflection on practice. As we have seen in all previous chapters, the values and attitudes that are held, the nature and purpose of the investigation, the environment and participants, all influence the research instruments employed. Chapter 3 has explained and demonstrated practitioner investigation consistent with the ethnographic investigative approaches often referred to as the 'interpretative paradigms' (Denscombe, 2010; Mukherji and Albon, 2010). This chapter outlines creative approaches to research activities that will be suited to similarly small-scale work-based investigation which:

- is carried out within the community of the setting and involves the feelings, responses and behaviours of those involved;
- involves the researcher being fully involved with the project as an insider;

- is focused on identifying the factors that influence the lived experience of those involved and the ways that the experience can be enhanced through change and development of practice;
- involves the personal and professional reflection of the researcher as they consider the stories and lives shared in the research process;
- is usually framed around an interpretation of qualitative data rather than focused on a statistical and mathematical analysis of 'objective' responses.

The chapter is illustrated with reference to reflections from practitioner studies and the methods that informed them. In addressing the novice researcher directly, it invites a reflective response towards decision-making in local contexts. It highlights the need to be clear on the purpose of investigation in order to identify appropriate methods and signposts further reading from established academic texts. It examines various approaches to working with and engaging children and adults as co-researchers in a way that will give all concerned ownership of practice. This contrasts with the idea that the researcher already has all the answers and is just using the research activity to 'check out' their own expertise and knowledge. Instead, it considers the 'real-world' research of practitioners as discussed in Chapter 2, consistent with the notions of communities of learning and practice emerging from the work of Wenger (1998) and explored in Chapter 7. To clarify terminology: 'instruments', 'activities' and 'methods' are used interchangeably to represent the discussion of our colleagues in other parts of the text.

What is the purpose of your study?

When articulating the 'research problem', it is helpful to organise your thinking in terms of the three 'purposes' of investigation recognised by Clough and Nutbrown (2002) – are you 'exploring', 'explaining' or 'predicting' aspects of practice? The extended examples provided in the chapter are intended to illustrate how such investigations develop 'on the ground':

- *Exploratory*. Alison's investigation (Jackson, 2008 unpublished) was an exploration of the concept of 'quality' and the different perspectives of quality apparent in political (policy), parent and practitioner perceptions.

- *Explanatory*. Sue's initial study (Callan, 2007 unpublished) tried to explain the emotional dimensions of adult learning in order to plan for the development of reflective dispositions in experienced practitioners. For her study (Davies, 2007 unpublished), Tracy was convinced that greater use of information and communications technology (ICT) in the school literacy hour would promote children's engagement and involvement. She sought methods that enabled her to represent the children's experience in presenting proposals for development to her colleagues.

- *Predictive*. Aspects of Carole's study (Ellis, 2007 unpublished), featured extensively in Chapter 3, involved investigating fathers' involvement in community groups in order to try and anticipate the success of new activity groups for which she was responsible.

The selection of meaningful research activities is best achieved if the *purpose* of the study is clear from the outset. The studies represented here show how creative approaches to research activities have added value to the outcome of investigation and the ability to reflect on practice and change. Most investigations will ultimately involve a range of methods with elements of all three strands. If you are clear about your intentions and the purpose of the research activities they will be effective. Table 5.1 shows how different methods suit different purposes.

Table 5.1 Research activities to support practitioner investigation

Exploratory methods	Explaining methods	Predicting methods
• Focus group • Creative workshop discussions • Shared stories/autobiography • Journals	• Focus group • Peer observation	• Questionnaire • Interview • Survey
• Child tour • Child conference • Questionnaire	• Child observations • Video recording • Tape recording • Photography	• Children's drawings
• Peer observation • Literature review	• Survey • Interview	

The discussion of methods in the body of the chapter is based on exploratory or explanatory studies. However, this brief activity illustrates the relationship between purpose, method and sample in a predictive context:

Activity

Your waiting list for admissions is full to bursting and there is the opportunity to acquire a small building locally in order to split your provision over two sites. This is attractive as the new facility is nearer to the local school and shops, so you could extend your offer to include some after-school as well as day-care in the new premises. The Local Authority Development Officer suggests that you begin a feasibility study to predict interest and local need, prior to making the considerable commitment that such a change will involve.

- How might you predict the take-up of extra places?
- Where and how could you access a participant sample of possible 'customers'?
- How can you check on possible competition from other providers?
- From the methods grid in Table 5.1, highlight some useful research activities suited to your purpose.

How useful is a questionnaire to 'insider' investigation?

The questionnaire as it is commonly understood has a place in day-to-day practice and you will no doubt have used this format, perhaps when consulting with parents about proposals for new session times, menu planning or preferences about outings. For 'research' purposes, it is considered attractive because it is perceived as 'objective' and interpretation of responses can be represented numerically. It also appears to save time, as it does not involve direct researcher participation. Established texts (Roberts-Holmes, 2005) provide extensive guidance on the construction and use of questionnaires as a relatively quick, easy and efficient way of getting the sort of information that will stand alone – once you have weathered the process of ensuring that it is going to be effective in providing data that is useful to your project (Denscombe, 2010; Mukherji and Albon, 2010). In terms of the activity above, the questionnaire has a place in small-scale investigations and this is recognised in terms of managing the resulting 'data' and presenting findings in Chapter 6.

However, in terms of the identifiable characteristics of practitioner investigation, the questionnaire is limited as a method. How often have you been confronted with a form offering one or two choices of response and thought, 'well, it depends ... because ...'? Other methods can offer opportunity for respondents to think about and give detail of how they *feel* and why those feelings may be tied up with responses to experience beyond the setting but which will impact on the way your practice is perceived. Investigation to inform critical reflective practice involves the recognition that the setting is just one part of the lives and environments experienced by our colleagues as well as children and families. It is essential to accommodate this wider experience in your investigation if you want a realistic picture of the dynamics impacting on your practice. Alison recognised this when reflecting on her research design:

> I found it very hard to draw up a suitable questionnaire and in the process I realised that it was unlikely that I would obtain the information I was really after by using this method. On reflection, to obtain the qualitative feedback I was hoping for, I think it would have been beneficial to carry out face-to-face interviews with parents as well. However, this would have involved a much greater commitment of time, which I simply did not have so I continued to base my research on these questionnaires even though I acknowledge that this was not the best means to obtain the required data. Roberts-Holmes ... supports this view as he claims that: 'Questionnaires can only ever provide part of the answer to your overall research questions (2005: 142).' (Jackson, 2008 unpublished: 15–16)

Note how Alison's reflection brings out the importance of using a range of activities (triangulation – see Chapter 6) – and allowing time for investigating and reflecting on practice. Management and prioritising time is a major challenge, as she notes that use of interviews is a costly time commitment. Working practitioners tend to perceive themselves as 'time poor' but, as Alison found, time planning is important for the overall quality of outcomes. The purpose of practitioner investigation should be to facilitate and promote continuous quality improvement through reflective practice. This does demand time and we argue that it is time well spent.

Methods and participants – identifying your research 'sample' in design

Similarly, the three investigative strands will also point you in the direction of relevant participants, that is those who are most likely to provide you with meaningful 'data' for your investigation – commonly referred to in most texts as the 'research sample'.

For example, Alison's sample was 'ready-made' as it involved parents in her setting, but she needed to beware of 'convenience' sampling (Hayes, 2001). She was aware of a possible sample bias towards those parents who are more likely to engage in the process. Simple solutions such as putting the children's names into a box and asking another member of staff to draw out the required number of names can offer more inclusive sampling methods. Alison's study also extended to other settings so the sample size was enhanced.

As we have seen in Chapter 3, Carole's challenge as an outreach worker (Ellis, 2007 unpublished), was the need to find particular, relevant environments to generate her participant 'sample' of fathers, and to explore with them ways to initiate and support sustained involvement in parenting groups. Activities included discussions with fathers-to-be at ante-natal classes and visiting a Fathers Direct conference, so while participants were not within her immediate community of practice, they were entirely appropriate for her project.

Being brave about your methods (co-constructing the research)

Every day as a professional practitioner you promote the creative thinking and imagination of children. You advocate risk-taking, self-expression and personal challenge as a way of learning and yet, in adult practice, may sometimes opt for 'safety' and the familiar in order to get things 'right'. We hope that at this stage, you will be clearer that what seems familiar or safe in terms of research design may not suit your individual investigation or your position as a researcher explained in the earlier chapters.

If we take Alison's experience (Jackson, 2008 unpublished) as a working example, it is possible to identify other ways of conducting what was already an extremely successful study – and resolving the 'problems' she identified in her critical reflection. Her 'problem' was that interviews would take too much time – they are also fraught with complexity about the tendency of the interviewer to unconsciously influence the responses. How could you overcome this issue and use a method that might enable you to 'lead by following', that is to deflect attention from your role as 'the expert/leader' and to recognise participants as co-researchers rather than the 'subjects' of investigation?

Working with adults

Methods suited to exploratory investigations will try and put adults at ease, taking the spotlight away from individuals so that everyone feels able to participate. This strategy outlined here builds on the recognised value of creative groups discussed by Callan and Morrall (2009), but also represent close application of early childhood philosophies and traditions as part of practice drawn from Reggio Emilia (Abbot and Nutbrown, 2001) and Te Whariki (Carr and May, 2000) in particular.

Sometimes you take on the role of observer and 'scribe' – to remove yourself from the dynamic of conversation so that participant responses can be reasonably spontaneous and represent a shared experience. The concept of an activity-based conversation is taken from therapeutic counselling approaches (Callan and Morrall, 2009), but is effective in facilitating thoughtfulness by presenting an opportunity to first quieten the mind. Rather like written observations, the discussion is 'recorded' (maybe on tape or in a journal) and the interpretation of it checked back with participants to ensure that their meanings have not been distorted. Such methods are sound for use with parents and colleagues as participant groups. Nutbrown writes:

> A key difference between focus group interviews and focus conversation research is that, with the former, the role of participants often ends with the completion of data collection. For me, focussed conversations can continue to involve participants in the development of data to analysis and reporting. (Clough and Nutbrown, 2002: 79)

This is represented in the following picture of practice from a research project:

> My investigation focused on student experiences as both learners and senior practitioners, so there was a lot of scope for very powerful discussion of 'stories'. I did two creative activities: one involved a sensory activity (each member made a 'garden' from some soil and natural materials I brought in) – for the other, I gave cut-outs of handprints and the group decorated these while talking. I made notes but guided the discussion by putting into the ring some pre-prepared discussion points for exploration that I had written on postcards. Initially, these were issues I had taken from my literature search and then in later groups, bringing back some of the comments from earlier discussion or journals in order to see if they represented a common experience. This method meant that the group had control over the extent of personal information

disclosed, but I kept some kind of focus and impetus to discussion if it flagged. I didn't use a tape recorder, I just noted in my journal some key 'quotable quotes' so that I could write up the activity report later on. My interpretative records were checked with the group, but in this process I was already reflecting on outcomes in order to analyse implications for my future practice. It was fully my intention that as the study evolved, the group would be involved in the development of new ideas for delivery of the course. This would seem to be consistent with the framework for an effective study – a spiral of reflection and action resulting from a consistency of values, beliefs, the research question, methods and outcomes. (Adapted from Callan, 2007 unpublished)

The use of focused conversation as a method is recognised as part of the feminist research perspectives described by McCart-Neilsen (1990) and designed to empower participants. It is selected intentionally to avoid a personal interview, which is unlikely to generate uninhibited reflection because of the power dynamics described in the case study in Chapter 1 (Foster, 2008 unpublished).

Journals – autobiography as research

To extend the theme of sharing stories, many practitioners are in the habit of keeping a journal to support reflective practice. This is a personal 'space' where it is possible to thoroughly explore your own feelings and responses to the challenges and emotional dimension of work in the early childhood sector. Such journals have also been invaluable for practitioners trying to focus on the exact nature of an investigation. Writing and keeping your own journal (Bolton, 2005) also allows you to think more deeply about the issues underpinning the research question and early phases of the fieldwork, as identified in this reflection:

I carried ideas for my study round in my head for ages but I couldn't find my 'start point'. Eventually, I decided to just write down my own professional development story to see what came out of it. This was really useful because I could 'see' a number of external influences that had come together to impact on my decisions – much more than internal issues of my own. This set off a strand in reading for the literature review and generated the final decisions about how I would conduct the investigation. In the event, I shared my written story with the participant group and hoped it would prompt some useful feedback in starting our discussion. At the very least I was able to establish a culture in the investigation of personal sharing and openness because I had shown a willingness to divulge very personal information. (Adapted from Callan, 2007 unpublished)

Surveys

Rather like the way that keeping a journal was used in this example, surveys can serve a useful purpose in informing your decisions about how to progress an investigation. Mukherji and Albon (2010) provide clear guidance on using surveys as a research method in terms of their value to generating quantitative data – here we select *one* aspect of a survey in order to demonstrate its significance to a qualitative study.

A descriptive survey is a useful way of finding out information about experience and attitudes which will inform your decisions about *further exploratory/explanatory* investigative methods. The activity concerning market research is an appropriate scenario for surveying local provision – you might 'survey' the local authority website. In the context of Carole's initial practical problem of access to participants, an informal survey was found to be helpful:

> *Sure Start Children's Centres: Phase Three Planning and Delivery* (DFES, 2007b) identifies that working with fathers is one of five priorities for all centres. Centres must have a strategy to publicise services to fathers and to communicate why their involvement will benefit their children and themselves. It was my responsibility to progress our work as a team in this respect and to establish our own fathers group specifically. We were attracting a handful of fathers to some of the sessions we run and *I consulted with them* [our emphasis] and found that there was a fathers' group already well established and run by the Baptist church. (Adapted from Ellis, 2007 unpublished)

Note that Carole is describing external drivers for quality improvement and development of established good practice in the motivation for her investigation. What is also apparent is that she 'surveyed' the current service users for specific information. This was informal and achieved through spontaneous conversation in the centre and with people who became involved in the research in their own right – but here they contribute their expertise in assisting Carole to access more participants. Local practitioner networks offer a useful source for such 'surveys'.

Crucially, Carole wanted to ensure that her investigation was based on fathers' voices and not mediated through others. The initial contact with the church group offered the basis of further involvement with other men's groups over a large rural area and, effectively, resolved the initial practical barrier to a meaningful study.

Other practitioners will also 'survey' in the digital world in order to inform their study. Such use of the Internet is demonstrated in Chapter 1, with specific notes on ethical practice. In Chapter 4, due regard is given to accreditation of sites used so that information contributing to the investigation is credible and has some academic validity. This rigour must extend to the use of any statistical information gleaned from digital sources. For example, the demographic features of the local population in the community of the setting are often cited in locally based research reports with the intention of demonstrating the 'needs' of children and families. In any research report critical appraisal of such sources is necessary when analysing outcomes of the investigation. Denscombe (2010) in particular gives a clear evaluative framework for use of the Internet in research investigations.

Interviews and 'recorded' conversation – working without a clipboard

Carole's study is discussed at length in Chapter 3. She chose to conduct her interviews to maximise the possibility of engagement and minimise the things that would get in the way of effective communication. We have noted that Carole's interviews were open and unstructured, and that she did not take notes, carried no tape recorder and wrote up themes and issues as a journal record to support her interpretation. A number of visits to each group enabled her to check her interpretations with those involved:

> I had to consider the practicalities of how much time I had to undertake the research and what methods of accumulating evidence from fathers was the most appropriate. I would need to attend several sessions if I was to effectively achieve this so it was imperative that I gave myself plenty of time.

> My aim was to remain honest and open and discuss with the fathers their thoughts, opinions and ideas. I spoke with many men about their thoughts regarding fathers groups, and was very aware that I did not want to influence their responses, I wanted to gather information that will assist me to solve theoretical and practical problems and aid me to implement evidence-based practice. I question whether a 'scientific' approach can be used to ascertain these facts. As I engaged with each of the fathers I found a different approach was required. I had to rely on my personality, sensitivity and professional judgement to exact the information I required. (Adapted from Ellis, 2007 unpublished)

What is apparent here are recurring themes from the chapter so far – the need to allow time, the need to recognise that the quality of relationships and communication lie at the heart of a credible practitioner investigation, that the traditional emphasis on 'scientific enquiry' is recognised as restricting meaningful outcomes for practitioner investigation. If you are investigating people and social processes, relational and emotional sensitivity has to be represented in your methods (Pilcher, 2009). Self-awareness will enable you to consider your own strengths in terms of effective and assertive communication skills; however, the benefits of an informal approach are underlined in this experience:

> At one of the groups visited, I found that there was a BBQ in full swing with partners and children in attendance. The fathers had charge of the session, but happily informed me about issues they have encountered and how they seek guidance and support at the centre and from each other. They also suggested that, once our group got going, they could visit and establish a cross-county contact. (Ellis, 2007 unpublished: 16)

This informal setting enabled the fathers themselves to communicate freely and to introduce to Carole an outcome for future practice that had not previously been considered. The cultural and social act of sharing food can be useful for breaking down many barriers – it could be used as an effective strategy of providing for comfort needs if you aim to engage positively with adults.

Inclusion – involving parents from cultural and language groups

As an ethical requirement of practice, inclusion is noted in Chapter 1. This has many facets but by recognising communication as fundamental to relational methods for investigation, it is important that we briefly extend discussion to consider the needs of families who have English as an additional language (EAL). It is not unusual in many areas of the four nations of the UK to find monolingual practitioners seeking ways to include and involve bi- and multi-lingual families. Rose Drury (2007) found that families were keen that children retained their first language as part of their home culture, but had high expectations for them as achievers in the educational system. This motivation for achievement can be a source for families' positive engagement with any action to develop practice in settings. However, such is the diversity of language communities in areas of the UK that practitioners have had to become very creative in accessing support for their practice. It is not always the case that parents are the first port of call here. Sensitivity to the relative strengths in English language use of fathers and mothers is a requirement – in some communities women may be monolingual and engaging with fathers or older siblings of the children is a strategy for supporting practice if you cannot access formal support from teaching/language assistants. Having carefully considered any ethical or safeguarding limitations, colleagues in practice have used support from local employers (Japanese), further education colleges (for students who can assist with a range of Asian languages), local shops and even restaurants (Portuguese/Italian/Polish) to access language communities for translation purposes in order to construct questionnaires, surveys and support parent interviews or discussion groups – with the added benefit of community engagement beyond the confines of the setting.

Work with children

Discussion concerning methods for working with children in practitioner research is also included in Chapter 1. As an experienced practitioner, it is possible that you will feel more at home with observation methods and use of recording equipment for work with children as part of the curriculum management, delivery, reflection and design in your setting. Here, we consider the possibilities for integrating this expertise into work-based investigation supported further by the use of a Mosaic 'toolkit' as developed by Alison Clark (2004). The points made earlier about creative activities enabling participants to express themselves with as little constraint as possible and to be involved as an 'expert' in their own experience applies to children. Clark's methods have the added dimension of enabling the child to articulate and represent their feelings and responses to practice in a way that promotes involvement for even the youngest service users. More recently, the work of Armistead (2008) gives further attention to children's perspectives and this offers further insight into their ability to act as strong participants in enquiries which focus essentially on the quality of their experience.

As we have seen, the mosaic of methods include observations, child tours, drawings, mapping and photographs (all of which can be used with individuals) and child conferencing/consultation (which can facilitate small-group discussion). Parents can be involved in conferencing in a way that enables them to comment and provide further insight into the child's response. The idea is that by combining different strategies for engaging the child/ren (triangulation), the data generated for your investigation is significantly more meaningful. For instance, if one child's tour reveals that s/he is frightened by some areas of the playground, a conference involving one or two others will provide the opportunity to identify whether this is a representative response or the result of individual experience.

Indeed, the Mosaic approach is genuinely exploratory in that it is difficult for the practitioner to anticipate the outcome. For example, some practitioners have investigated areas of the environment that are significant to the child using the child-led tour. It has been sobering to find that a carefully resourced area is avoided as a place that is 'too noisy'!

Engaging children in research is consistent with rights-based practice and child-centred principles within the Early Years Foundation Stage (EYFS) (DCSF, 2008a). It also enables practitioners to represent and explain children's responses to other adults from an informed position and can contribute to our professional position as advocate for the child's interests. To illustrate these themes, we focus on the use of observations and child conferencing in a school classroom.

Observations and child conferencing

In the design of her investigation, Tracy (Davies, 2007 unpublished) was seeking ways to represent and explain the children's experience to her colleagues as part of improving practice in the use of ICT to support classroom literacy activities. Because the study focuses on the experience of children in the curriculum, it is vital that they are represented in the investigation. As part of her literature review, Tracy discovered that use of ICT resources also encourages quiet children and bi-lingual learners to participate with confidence in classroom activities, so there was good reason to conduct the investigation utilising the equipment she wished to promote. In an informal survey of colleagues on her course, Tracy also gained information about the use of ICT in other settings and could use this to inform her methods and her reflection on findings. Again, note how the various strands of investigation work in a dynamic relationship together – teamwork and partnership was also significant to this study:

> I planned two activities to be completed within the literacy hour over several lessons. Both involved small group work – one activity involved the use of ICT to produce a story animation for presentation to the class, and the other was to discuss and write down a story to tell. While the children were completing these activities I conducted written observations and then compared the two observations to see how long they stayed focused.

> I also spoke to the children in small groups about how they felt about using ICT in lessons. I had initially planned to send questionnaires out to the children in the class, but decided against this as I felt the children might have the vocabulary to express what they feel, but not have the knowledge to be able to write it down. So I felt that talking to them in small focus groups rather than one to one, as I felt that they might feel slightly intimidated by this, would be a better way of getting their true feelings about ICT. (Davies, 2007 unpublished: 6)

It is not surprising that Tracy's findings from the child conference all point to the fact that children enjoy ICT, they want to explore and find out about it, and it holds their concentration and motivates them – if the task is fun, exciting and achievable. In fact, their 'work' on the animation projects continued into discussion at playtime and a willingness to work through lunchtime as well! This raised for Tracy and her colleagues the opportunity to reflect on the role of the adult in facilitating ICT within the setting. They examined their own competence, confidence, experience and knowledge and sought to implement ICT in a way that will motivate and engage the children and value their expertise – again demonstrating the dynamics of the research and reflection process. Tracy's own reflection included the efficacy of her methods:

> When I started this project I felt that I couldn't see the end and didn't know which direction to turn. I'm glad I picked this topic to look at, because it has shown me that my views and beliefs were correct and has given me the confidence to push the use of ICT within my setting more. As a result, I have been given the responsibility of implementing ICT to Key Stage 1, and have one afternoon a week to teach the children ICT skills. As for the research activities, I feel that talking to colleagues and children was a better way of gaining the information I needed, as if I had handed out questionnaires I might not have got as much information back, especially with the children as the answers would probably have been yes or no. (Davies, 2007 unpublished: 10–11)

 ## Summary

This brings our discussion for the chapter in a full circle as Tracy acknowledges the limitations of the questionnaire for qualitative studies. In all examples from practice, there may have been alternative methods available. In Tracy's study for example, it may have been effective to video the children's activities and ask them to commentate on them in the conference, but the point here is to decide whether this would have really affected the quality of final investigative outcomes. Generally speaking, for small-scale work-based investigation, if all the features of the research process are aligned in an investigation, and a range of strategies used to gather 'data', then the outcome should be authentic in terms of the specific community of practice – the findings should enable us to progress the cycle of reflection to identify change and strategies for managing and leading settings. If, on reflection, we can see things that could have been more effective, this is a learning outcome for next time rather than a point of 'failure'.

Further reading

The following titles represent a selection of the texts that have informed our writing as practitioners and researchers.

Clark, A. (2004) 'The Mosaic approach and research with young children', in *The Reality of Research with Children and Young People*. London: Sage. This provides more substantial detail on the rationale and values underpinning the Mosaic toolkit.

Clough, P. and Nutbrown, C. (2007) *A Student's Guide to Methodology: Justifying Enquiry*, 2nd edn. London: Sage. This contains useful activities for exploring motivation for and values and purpose of investigation and supports informed decisions about methods.

Costley, C., Elliott, G. and Gibbs, P. (2010) *Doing Work-Based Research: Approaches to Enquiry for Insider Researchers*. London: Sage. A recent title which examines theory and practice for work-based investigation.

Section 3

Learning from Research

6

Identifying what has been found – explaining a new position

Sharon Smith with Michael Reed and Sue Callan

Chapter overview

This chapter examines the way evidence, or 'data', that comes from an investigation is interpreted. We consider why it is important to interpret what this evidence 'says', clearly and honestly, and to consider how such things as an ethical position might influence the analysis of data. The chapter draws on a number of approaches to help define and refine views and makes a case for seeing the whole process of research as a form of data gathering that needs to be rigorously interrogated before offering reflection on practice. The practice-based investigations used in the chapter are drawn from the experiences of Tracy (Davies, 2007 unpublished) and Alison (Jackson, 2008 unpublished). Tracy explored ways to improve the engagement of children in school through the use of information and communication technology (ICT), while Alison engaged in a collaborative examination of the notion of 'quality' in her pre-school community. Both practitioners were motivated to explore these areas by their personal values and beliefs as well as their professional experience and we would like to acknowledge that the investigations are representative of the 'organic' qualities of practice discussed in the editors' introduction.

In advance of our main content, we would like to pause for thought and reflect on the 'birth' of Chapter 6. This book is presented in both the introduction and Chapter 8 as representing our own research processes to support the evolution of the text from the 'vision' of a single person to a co-construction involving a number of contributors. This process has been intuitive for the most part but, within this, each chapter author has had to ensure academic rigour as well as presentation for a (largely) non-academic readership. Chapter 6 is a significant and important chapter because it is intended to bring together all the elements of a 'research project' introduced by our colleagues, but to discuss data analysis in a way that is consistent with the methodological position of the text overall. As a result it has been produced in many versions and subject to discussion and revision, in the process of which it became a co-constructed chapter. Our challenge has been to ensure that in this construction, each participant author 'voice' has been represented and each contribution recognised as adding value to this final version. For novice researchers and work-based practitioners, this models not only the tensions of ethical practice in research but the features of early years practice as a collaborative, supportive tradition based on the characteristics of social construction at the heart of learning.

Where does data come from?

Data starts to emerge alongside the focus for the research, even at the stage where this focus is just an embryonic idea, a view, a personal theory, a practice improvement goal or even a hypothesis. For example, a setting held a meeting to discuss an aspect of practice and at that meeting it was decided that the 'team' would try to do things differently and evaluate what went on. It could be argued that there is evidence (data) which suggested that change was a positive part of the ethos of the setting. This is because the meeting itself tells us that there exists a culture of 'openness' of staff and management to consider quality and change. It also tells us that 'purpose' had a practical meaning for all those involved as we have discussed in Chapter 2. It can sometimes also mean a deeper purpose about trying to understand a subject, an action or a theoretical position. While Tracy and Alison, as practitioner researchers, gathered information and engaged in their research they had already started to consider ways of looking at 'data'. This is because they were looking at changes in practice, their own assumptions and a consideration of what they saw through being an 'insider', in effect a consideration of their personal and professional values, beliefs and position. This may appear somewhat different to an accepted view of what data looks like. We recently asked students 'what do you see as data?' They said it was 'information collected', 'a collection of tables of information', 'statistics', 'factual evidence' – none of which are 'wrong', but tell us that there is a tendency to see 'data' as the way results are presented rather than where it comes from, the process involved and what it will be used for. This resonates more completely with a view that data result from a systematic recording of information, both process and product. Data *analysis* on the other hand involves working to uncover patterns and trends in the data; it also involves interpreting the data and explaining those patterns and trends. When this goes on, any interpretation is influenced by background knowledge and experience and sometimes by being part of the setting within which the data was obtained as well as its purpose. By publishing or presenting their data practitioners can explain the techniques they used to analyse and interpret that data, and give their audience the opportunity to both review the data and use it to inform and develop future research. It may then have a direct impact and influence upon practice.

Data is then examined

Previous chapters have considered ways to collect data, using particular methods that are fit for the purpose of investigating practice in an early years setting. They also considered the need to have a strong ethical framework. Assuming that these aspects of the research are in place and that sound preparatory work has been done, then a clear range of data should emerge. Having said this we must stress the need to have a proactive, purposeful and well planned project. Doing so will enhance the quality of the data that is retrieved and this is a key point. It is the quality of the data that is important, not necessarily the volume nor a need to compare and contrast a large number of settings. Data can equally emerge from a small-scale project looking at what you do well, finding out why and recommending further improvement. Therefore by 'quality' we mean data that has emerged from a variety of sources, that has been owned by those most closely involved in the process and willingly shared with you as a researcher: data that when analysed may lead to improvement in practice. Your task is then quite simple: it is to make sense of this information – which might be different viewpoints expressed by parents or a breakdown of the numbers of parents attending an event – and from this provide analysis. It then becomes possible to make a recommendation for you and others to perhaps change practice. You may then decide to publish this as part of an award at a college or university or informally through a presentation to the setting. For example, Tracy reported informally to her colleagues in school but had to formulate a formal report for her Foundation Degree Award (FdA). Alison used similar methods, reporting informally through a presentation to colleagues on the FdA, producing her formal academic report and extending this for publication in Reed and Canning (2010). Tracy used written forms of representation but Alison's discussion also used graphs. Other projects have utilised diagrams and pictures to support the explanation of data. Indeed this transformation of information can itself form part of the analysis of data as the researcher offers a written explanation and analysis about what they have found. Analysis is the process of writing to represent a thoughtful response to the outcomes through comparing, contrasting and evaluating. Clough and Nutbrown, in recognising how to report the findings from any investigation, make the point that 'writing is essential for viewing our thinking' (2007: 183), because it helps us to reflect and to discover what we want to say. As we do this we are taking the opportunity to evaluate a given area of practice or experience (especially ethnographic studies, as shown in Chapter 3) and identify an issue, an intervention or recommendation (Robson, 2002). Data allows us to consider explanations, reasons, or suggestions for a new approach derived from the outcome of the investigation. The process of reporting requires that this evidence be 'represented' and explained through analysis and interpretation of the wider features of the investigation – the values and attitudes and the knowledge base, as well as the social and political contexts. As long as the report identifies what was found, explains and interprets 'meaning' for the setting and proposes action as a result, then it will be fit for purpose. 'Findings' (as shown in Chapter 3 through exploration of an ethnographic study) might be identified in a thematic manner: data is examined to identify and categorise themes and key issues that 'emerge' from it. Through a careful analysis of their data, using this inductive process, ethnographers generate tentative theoretical explanations from their empirical work.

In understanding what data looks like, we can see that photographs represent an alternative representation, as do diagrams. For example, look back to the introduction to the book and find Figure 1. This represents the elements and interrelatedness of integrated working as well as the drivers for change towards multi-professional practice. It gives another example of the different ways to represent issues, themes and concepts arising from research activities. Visual images as data representation are particularly useful when summarising

Figure 6.1   Representing Olivia's digital landscape at 12 weeks old

Reproduced from Reed and Canning *Implementing Quality Improvement and Change in the Early Years,* 2011, SAGE.

findings or to show an interrelationship between ideas, concepts or sequences of events. In the same way examples of children's work, pictures of artefacts or indeed video (on a digital memory stick) of changes made to the environment can be used. There are also digital forms of representation which Tyler (2011) uses as illustrated in Figure 6.1. The figure represents Linda's research on how young children perceive their developing 'digital worlds'. It is a technique that has the potential to form or develop analysis, and which is another facet of Linda's own doctoral research.

In all cases, a narrative is required to explain, or interpret, the intended meaning. Denscombe (2010) defines such interpretation as the recognition of patterns and regularities. This is important as it should not be up to the reader to immediately recognise and interpret data and findings; it is for the practitioner researcher to do this. When they do so, they should also be conscious of the 'audience' and the ethical reporting stance they hold. At one level this is to ensure that their interpretation provides an explanation in words and terms which can be understood. When we translate another language we provide an explanation/interpretation in our own words, so with this in mind the presentation of data requires sensitivity to those who shared in its construction and to whom it is disseminated. Data presented to participants such as colleagues, children or parents should be produced in a way which is meaningful and articulates the outcome of the research. It needs to be understandable to them and related to the questions asked, that is to be conscious of and recognise the needs of the audience. Participants will be seeking to ensure that their involvement has been represented fairly. The discussion in Chapter 1 argues that, ideally, a research project is a journey shared with the participants. At the stage of reporting, discussion of their responses and views should not just become data about them. As researchers we should therefore be sensitive to the ways we present participant views in reporting findings from the information collected. For example, Alison used the voices of a number of people in her study. She realised that some of this was meaningful to the participants. While it was not so significant for her as the researcher, it presented a truer 'picture' of the subject investigated and provided a representation of what others had disclosed (see Figure 6.2).

This technique illustrates that interrogating data is about explaining and interpreting what you find, not finding things to report: a truism highlighted by Denscombe (2010), who sees a need to recognise the importance of translating the meaning of the responses given without bias from our own perspectives. For instance, how does the researcher hear the voices of the participants and their intended meaning? Perhaps the answer is, as Blaxter et al. suggest 'that research requires professionalism and the researcher must pay attention to alternative values, views, meanings and explanations, while remaining alert to biases and distortion' (2001: 55). As such we must be alert to this in representing and discussing results. Hitchcock and Hughes (1995) confirm such dilemmas and identify the difficulties of recording 'voices' and how the interpretation of the data can distort the original meanings of the participants. The effective use of narrative text alongside the quantitative data presented within Alison's report overcame some of these challenges. She explains how her data collection and her interpretation of the data was owned by and shared with those who had a stake in the research. Both Alison and Tracy recognise and deal with the 'safeguarding' strategies noted in Chapter 1. They openly 'protect' their respondents without lessening the impact of what they had to say. They make clear the way they gathered and reported data with regard to professional propriety and ethical standpoints. However, it is useful to note they did not (within their settings)

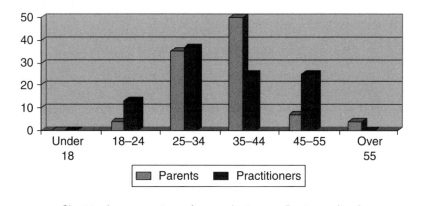

Chart to show percentage of respondents according to age bands

Only one practitioner thought that the quality of the service they offered was *not* a factor for parents when accessing their provision:

'No because it's part of a school LEA and free!'

and offered the following explanation for what they thought influenced parental choice of childcare:

'Our nursery is a feeder for the school, it is free and they want their children to be with their peer group for school. They very rarely question what we offer. We volunteer why we do things etc.'

Figure 6.2   Data representation and analysis in a report (Jackson, 2008: 20)

have a policy covering wider ethical issues for insider research – something that is given further attention and extended in Chapter 8. Such policies prevent the investigator being at risk and, in turn, the data and the interpretation of the data being at risk. Ethicality is also important for reflecting on professional credibility and development, as shown in this statement from Alison's work:

> By carrying out further research with the parents and the children and staff in my settings to obtain their perspectives, I would hope to combine both this 'bottom up' approach with the 'top down' approach and my constantly reflective practice to achieve more equality amongst all the stakeholders in our provision and, therefore, a truly inclusive, high quality provision. (Jackson, 2008 unpublished: 26)

Data

Data is the result of a process that starts with the position taken by a researcher; it has been influenced, touched, moulded and shaped – in part, by where and when it was gathered and in part by the methods and approaches used. In some ways it is restricted data, as ethical perspectives may have lessened what could be asked of children or parents. It will be the subject of scrutiny and seen though different eyes, by different audiences even before its results are known. Even then it may be criticised because it was only done in one place or in one way. It is therefore important that the researcher defends their position, carefully explains the route taken and completes rigorous data analysis. All of this we can see in Tracy's investigation which sought to identify whether the use of ICT motivated children to stay on task. This question was based on her knowledge and experience as an insider. She started by comparing children's reaction to planned activities designed to enhance engagement with ICT. This was in part shaped by her perspectives and professional values about how children should learn. This produced 'day-to-day data' which was interpreted and became the focus for further investigation. It prompted her to collect more varied data from a range of sources and situations – data likely to reveal a true picture of what was going on, so it had to reflect a number of perspectives. This allowed her to further interpret what was happening and, ultimately, influence future practice.

Its all sounds so linear, like a route from A to B. Yet this is not the case. The process masks a many-layered and complex pattern of thinking and interpretation. Denscombe (2010) sees this as the 'deconstruction' of data, which means adopting a critical approach to our own interpretation through searching for hidden messages, considering cultural aspects and formulating a 'conclusion'. This is achieved by 'interrogating' the data and thinking critically about the contexts from which it originates. Denscombe suggests this is a stance which requires the researcher to be an 'active, not passive, interpreter of message content' (2010: 287). Spradley (1979) offers some examples and asks us to consider the physical environment, the people involved, the activities that occurred, the key actions that take place and the timescale, as well as the sequence of events and in addition the aims of those involved and the emotional environment: all areas that an early years practitioner will recognise as being very important in order to understand the realities of practice. Of course this can lead to an accusation that the researcher is interpreting things in a way that suits their own perspectives or position – an aspect of interpretation which Carr argues is not simply unavoidable, rather it is essential: 'Partisanship is an essential ingredient in educational research whose elimination could only be achieved by eliminating the entire research enterprise itself' (2000: 439). Malcolm (1993), however, suggests that such a stance may lead to questionable practices in the selection, manipulation and interpretation of data. It can lead to 'unhealthy professional entrenchment' (1993: 144). She suggests a need to be reflective and self-critical in order to make explicit the evidence and arguments needed to defend a position. In that case, it would be reasonable to look at the relationship between data sources and the forms of data in order to offer reasonable and rigorous analysis. This approach is sometimes considered to be 'triangulation'. Denzin (1970) distinguished four forms of triangulation:

1. *Data triangulation* – several methods of sampling, at different times, social situations, on a variety of people.

2. *Investigator triangulation* – more than one researcher gathers and interprets data.

3. *Theoretical triangulation* – more than one theoretical position in interpreting data.

4. *Methodological triangulation* – using different methods to lessen confusion between data gathering methods methodological approaches.

Denzin (2006) refines these terms as 'within-method' triangulation, interpreted as varieties of the same method to investigate a research issue, and 'between-method' triangulation, more to do with contrasting research methods such as a questionnaire and observation. Sometimes triangulation is also taken to include a merging of quantitative and qualitative methods of investigation. More often it is used to indicate a cross-checking of findings, for example one method with another. It is also important to remember the *purpose* of triangulation. We see this as increasing the credibility of results to enhance the position and interpretation given to those results by the researcher. Cohen and Manion see the construct as an 'attempt to map out, or explain more fully ... human behavior by studying it from more than one standpoint' (2000: 254). Altrichter et al. propose that it gives a more detailed and balanced picture of the situation (2008: 147). O'Donoghue and Punch see triangulation as a 'method of cross-checking data from multiple sources' (2003: 78).

However, triangulation is also open to criticism (Cheng, 2005; Bogdan and Biklen, 2006). It is seen as something that confers on research a realism that says there is just one way of seeing the world. It is also argued that the world is socially constructed and it needs more than one interpretation of the situation under review. Another criticism is that some methods are beyond comparison, for example a focus group and a highly structured interview. Nevertheless, triangulation has a use for enhancing the credibility of a research account and it offers an opportunity to consider a blending of both qualitative and quantitative approaches.

Analysis

As data is explored it may highlight themes which merge and can therefore be analysed together. Patton (1987) has described this as 'content analysis'. He also refers to 'inductive analysis' where categories, themes and patterns may emerge and the presentation of results is concerned with any variation between them. Therefore there is a need to define terms, make comparisons, contrast information and evaluate what was found. Evaluation also needs to be seen in relation to contextual features. As seen in Chapter 4, this would include returning to the views of expert opinion from the literature. This is important because the data can be 'challenged' in terms of concerning with or offering a critique of accepted 'discourse'. It can also challenge policy documents and proposals which do not always rest within a 'research or enquiry base'. These increasingly appear on the Internet and care must be taken to explore them and again challenge some of their assumptions. This is indeed what critical interrogation requires and we need to recall what was said in Chapter 4 in terms of merging the 'preparation' of an investigation with its 'conclusion'. That means looking forward and back each step of the way, and it also means being honest. It means acknowledging that sometimes things did not work or did not succeed and saying why this was the case. Such 'failure' or 'constraint' is rarely reported as a 'definite' statement because it usually relates to one situation and may have succeeded with some slight modification or change in approach. There may have been design constraints in the way the investigation was planned and managed or in the range and scope of the data and methods used. Perhaps the data did not reveal what was expected, for example it did not provide sufficient information or revealed something that was not 'visible' at first glance. However, this does not have to be a problem. It can reveal interesting and new information – for example, that parents found an Internet social networking site more appealing and relevant to their needs than the formal organised group meeting at a children's centre. Your data might move you to think the same way and build on this 'other' research. As you are doing this, you are offering analysis and interpretation because they are intertwined, in which case you need to have in mind some precautionary questions. Of course, these are just as valid to consider at the start of the process as at the end.

Was the data gathered in a way that shows a process and an inter-relationship between ideas and thoughts at the start? Did these lead to an ethically based approach using methods of investigation that made every attempt to be fair, valid and reliable?

Overall did the data provide a realistic and honest basis for analysis and interpretation? Was the range and scope appropriate? Was it accurate and ethically strong?

Could you see social, political aspects in the data?

Could context, space, people and time be seen?

Were the voices of participants heard?

Is it possible to compare and contrast the data with other work in the same 'field'? Are there similarities which confirm your data is sound, much the same, different?

Can you identify similarities, contradictions and 'overlaps' from the data? Was it 'triangulated' in a way that gives it substance and can you realistically argue this was the case?

Does it alter your values and beliefs about the focus of the study?

Does it alter your position as a researcher?

Does it shed light on refining, defining, changing or adapting practice in terms of the focus of the investigation?

Can the data be shared and understood by others? Will it require 'translation' into graphs, figures, points, quotes or sections? (Remembering that by doing so you may impact upon analysis because you may be regrouping, organising and interrogating data in a different way).

You too are part of the data. What did you learn about yourself in the process? (Part of the discussion in Chapter 7.)

Summary

Costley et al. (2010) say that providing feedback and recommendations brings meaning and purpose to the research. Of course, this means linking data interpretation, analysis and findings. It means being honest, it means being accurate, it means being careful to report findings and not speculating too heavily on the 'what' and 'ifs'. It will be shared with others. This means asking, what might happen when I show people? How do I share materials? Who will be involved? What happens if the data reveals things that may cause concern or there is resistance to making specific recommendations? These are just some of the issues to be addressed when considering the impact of recommendations. They are ethical perspectives, which underline yet again the fact that ethicality runs all the way through the process. They are also questions which in themselves form 'data' – data about the impact of the study, and data that tells us about the inter-activity and process-based issues that are raised when we engage in insider, practice-based research. Unfortunately, there are no easy answers, other than honesty, ethicality and a proactive stance that has prepared the setting or those involved to receive the results and see themselves as part of the final state of an enquiry. It does, however, tell us that we are starting to close the theory–practice gap (Heron and Reason, 2001) by emphasising professional judgement within a climate of collaborative endeavour. As Goodfellow (2007) suggests, practice-based research enables practitioners to develop a greater appreciation of their professional practice and provides an increased opportunity to review and challenge the assumptions and values that underpin such practices.

Further reading

Data analysis is a complex area as it is inextricably tied to the debates on methodology noted in Chapter 2. We recommend some further reading for those studying at a level which requires a deeper engagement with the theory and practice of research.

An interesting website that contains varied materials all focusing on action research and surrounding issues is the following:

'Action Research Electronic Reader', online at: http://www.scu.edu.au/schools/gcm/ar/arr/arow/default.html.

The following website at the University of Birmingham contains important and perceptive papers from an ESRC Teaching and Learning Research Partnership Seminar Series, including work by Furlong and Oancea (2005) who offer critical reflection on ways to conduct and develop practice-based research and what this means in terms of the quality of research evidence:

http://www.education.bham.ac.uk/research/seminars1/esrc_4/index.shtml.

The following is a challenging article that considers 'discourse analysis' and brings the argument to bear for the researcher. It may be read in conjunction with the article by the same authors referenced in Chapter 7.

Tirado, F. and Gálvez (2007) 'Positioning theory and discourse analysis: some tools for social interaction analysis', *Forum Qualitative Sozialforschung/Forum: Qualitative Social Research*, 8 (2). online at: http://www.qualitative-research.net/fqs/

7

Repositioning yourself – personal and professional change through work-based investigation

Sue Callan, Linda Tyler and colleagues

Chapter overview

This chapter focuses on the *impact* of work-based investigation beyond the representation and discussion of 'findings' featured in Chapter 6. This impact will include personal and professional development for the researcher and the team in the setting, as well as enhanced practice 'outcomes' for children and families. It may also lead to the researcher repositioning themselves in their team within local communities of practice and making a contribution to wider professional networks within the sector. We demonstrate the impact of work-based research through an examination of change represented in the experiences of our colleagues, Carole Ellis, Alison Jackson, Tracy Davies, Sue Foster and Liz Olliver, whose unpublished projects have been featured throughout the text. The chapter offers a framework through which similarly experienced practitioners/inexperienced investigators can identify:

- how critical thinking drives change in reflective practice;
- how this is represented in reporting on research in 'formal' contexts; and

- the personal and professional changes that can emerge as a result of small-scale projects.

The featured projects are representative of the diverse roles and practice within the early childhood sector. These contributions enable us to consider examples of change and inform an understanding of the symbiotic relationship between research processes, reflective practice and quality improvement, in particular how reflection and reflexivity (Appleby, 2010) emerge as the result of investigating practice. Jude Simms in Chapter 4 has illustrated this journey in terms of the formative actions required for researching practice in teams, showing how awareness of the literature promotes greater engagement with 'discourse' beyond that of the setting in the wider context for practice. This chapter charts the journey in terms of the evolving discourse (positioning in relation to theory and practice) in local teams which is research-informed. It identifies the impact of research and critical reflection on personal and professional 'outcomes' and the qualities required to lead practice in a national context.

Work-based investigation and leading practice

Reflection involves looking back in order to move forward, so it is helpful at this point to take stock of some of the other themes offered in this text with regard to the various 'positions' of the researcher.

- The editors' introduction and Chapter 2 show that work-based projects can be understood as a meaningful part of traditional, 'formal' theories of academic research and knowledge acquisition/ transfer (discourse). While 'informal' investigations undertaken as part of senior practitioner responsibility for improving quality of provision may be small-scale, localised and centred on a specific community of practice, they are no less important for that. As a feature of the professional role at the forefront of social welfare responsibilities for work with children and families, informal research underpins our interpretation, understanding and implementation of statutory requirements.

- Such projects also support the development of senior practitioners, the quality of provision and the development of team and collaborative approaches to practice as required by the legislative and policy framework for care and learning. These qualities are a feature of the discussion of ethical practice in Chapter 1 (where Alison's project (Jackson, 2008 unpublished) on parent perceptions of 'quality' and Sue's (Foster, 2008 unpublished) investigation into her colleagues' perceptions of reflective practice are both featured). The impact of the investigations discussed in earlier chapters, is representative of the professionalisation of the workforce.

- Chapter 3 explains that work-based investigation characterised by the close involvement of the researcher represents the features conventionally applied to ethnographic research paradigms, where the practitioner is *inside* the process (a distinction clarified by Costley et al. (2010)). The discussion about ethnographic methods (or 'instruments') is illustrated by an examination of Carole's community development study (Ellis, 2007 unpublished) to promote the involvement of fathers in local groups.

- Other examples are found in Chapter 4 in which the impact on local policies is identified from the investigations into healthy snacks and improving transition. Jude Simms demonstrates that the investigation of literature (including research projects), policy frameworks and practice strategies for the sector is a part of the day-to-day process of managing and leading the improvement of children's experience in settings. It is also the means by which lead practitioners continue to update their own knowledge and professional development in the role and consequently to support the continued development of others.

- In Chapter 6 we are reminded that any project requires a reporting process and Sharon Smith explores how this might be conducted in settings, from a consideration of the point at which the investigator 'starts' the project, to the process of identifying what has been found out and how the impact of this might represent a 'new' position that will facilitate the consideration of change discussed here.

All authors have discussed investigation as linked to the day-to-day role of practitioners working with children and families, while at the same time offering the reflective 'space' for teams to identify new 'positions' which are accommodated by strategies to improve practice.

Figure 7.1 presents an illustration of the concept of 'positioning' oneself alongside the various sequences of researching. The process represented in the centre of the diagram links to specific chapters.

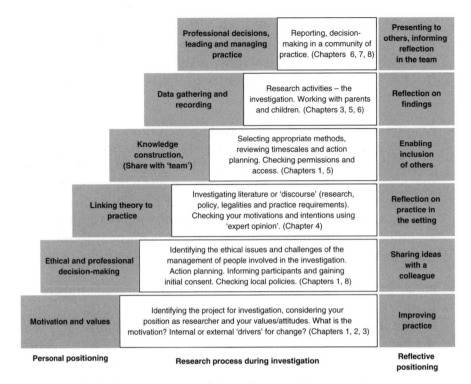

Professional decisions, leading and managing practice	Reporting, decision-making in a community of practice. (Chapters 6, 7, 8)	Presenting to others, informing reflection in the team
Data gathering and recording	Research activities – the investigation. Working with parents and children. (Chapters 3, 5, 6)	Reflection on findings
Knowledge construction, (Share with 'team')	Selecting appropriate methods, reviewing timescales and action planning. Checking permissions and access. (Chapters 1, 5)	Enabling inclusion of others
Linking theory to practice	Investigating literature or 'discourse' (research, policy, legalities and practice requirements). Checking your motivations and intentions using 'expert opinion'. (Chapter 4)	Reflection on practice in the setting
Ethical and professional decision-making	Identifying the ethical issues and challenges of the management of people involved in the investigation. Action planning. Informing participants and gaining initial consent. Checking local policies. (Chapters 1, 8)	Sharing ideas with a colleague
Motivation and values	Identifying the project for investigation, considering your position as researcher and your values/attitudes. What is the motivation? Internal or external 'drivers' for change? (Chapters 1, 2, 3)	Improving practice
Personal positioning	**Research process during investigation**	**Reflective positioning**

Figure 7.1   Building blocks for investigating practice

The right-hand side identifies reflective positioning points that assist collaborative work during an investigation. Personal positioning points to the left-hand side show the internal dialogue at the heart of learning from investigation. We return to these personal points when we identify the impact of study later in the chapter, so that the diagram can be used for both planning and review ('before' and 'after') activities.

The various building blocks for investigation are necessary in terms of managing the formal research process, but are interdependent for reflective practice. As a result the different blocks will each influence the overall construction at different times – not necessarily representing 'steps' but much more like a climbing frame in an interrelated sequence. A work-based investigation should gradually evolve as the practitioner researcher reflects on experience of the various sequences involved. Crucially, you can remain in control of an investigation that evolves in this way as long as the firm foundations and features of methodology presented by the building blocks are aligned in your project design.

Activity

Can you identify from Tracy's account below how the motivation for her study indicates the initial process for investigation as represented in Figure 7.1? Her personal position is shown here in terms of motivation and values, as is the driver to improve practice. The current discourse is identified with national frameworks and there is a long-term goal of personal professional development.

> For my research topic I looked at the use of Information and Communications Technology (ICT) within the literacy hour (as the government has laid down in the National Literacy Strategy (DfES, 1998)) and whether it motivates the children to stay on task. The children I work with are seven and eight year olds. I chose this topic because I have an interest in ICT and enjoy using it; I also took ICT as an exam at GCSE level and passed with a distinction. I would like to progress to become a primary school teacher, and thought that finding out whether ICT makes a difference to the children learning would be very useful for me later on in my chosen career. The use of ICT within literacy was also one area that a recent OFSTED inspection identified for improvement ... I believe that as childcare professionals we have an obligation to give the children in our care the best possible start in life. (Adapted from Davies, 2007 unpublished)

What is clear from Tracy's contribution is that she is engaging in a critical appraisal of practice in order to initiate change. Harris (1998) recognises that effective practice is linked to enquiry, reflection and continuous professional growth and it is to these features of criticality that we now turn.

Critical thinking, reflective practice and change

Work-based research provides practitioners with the ability to identify, with some level of certainty, whether earlier decisions about practice have been effective in implementation. Reflection does not afford the same opportunities to assess impact as research does; however, we cannot research effectively if we cannot reflect and we cannot reflect without the theoretical understanding that comes with researching. This endorses the argument presented at the heart of this book: the interconnectedness of formal and informal investigations in terms of the insights, skills and qualities generated by experience of 'research' however defined. Reflection and research are shown in Figure 7.1 to be part of a chronology of thought and action – other authors consider cyclical or spiral processes, each responding to the outcomes of reflection in action, on action and experience of practice as discussed by Schön (1983, 1987). Personal and professional development relies on the ability to critically appraise research findings in order to identify the impact on practice, i.e. the change that will result. It is therefore helpful to be clear about what is meant by 'criticality'.

Webster-Wright (2009) notes that continuing to learn and develop professionally to improve outcomes for children and ourselves is a universally accepted part of sector discourse and expected by early childhood practitioners and other stakeholders across all professions. Scriven and Paul (1987) have defined critical thinking as the intellectually disciplined process of actively and skilfully conceptualising, applying, analysing, synthesising and/or evaluating information gathered from – or generated by – observation, experience, reflection, reasoning or communication (i.e. 'research') as a guide to belief and action. Reflection requires high levels of critical thinking; when undertaking 'formal' projects in higher education this is made explicit through stated learning outcomes which ask students to 'critically reflect'. Often the use of 'critically reflect' is misunderstood and taken to mean thinking based on giving criticism or being critical of something and/or someone, whereas the term 'critical thinking' is used in research literature to describe reasonable, reflective thinking that focuses on task, people or belief (Ennis, 1993) – the context of the practice researched. In other words, critical thinking cannot be achieved unless we are prepared to think about our thinking (often called 'metacognition') and the social and cultural dynamics this involves. This is consistent with Finlay and Gough's definition of reflexivity as 'self-aware analysis' (2003: 9). Without critical thinking, there will be no outcome from reflection. When reflecting on our learning from investigation, the prime question will not be 'what was found' (which is the business of 'reporting'), but 'will it inform change' – both personal and professional within the setting. In other words, how *useful* has this investigation been? This is apparent in Carole's powerful reflection on personal and professional 'positioning' and the existence of a 'product' at the end of the process.

Engaging in this small-scale research project has given me the opportunity to extend my professional development to the wider context. By scrutinising my personal beliefs, my knowledge about gender issues, the socio-political arena, cultural norms, working hours, and allowing time for 'tuning in' are all issues that I have explored and I recognise create barriers to paternal engagement. Research has aided my understanding and I hope my ability to form positive strategies to overcome the constraints that inhibit paternal engagement and allow me to offer opportunities to enhance engagement. I have developed my professional and leadership skills by producing an information pack that I will make available to colleagues at the Children's Centre. (Ellis, 2007 unpublished: 26)

It appears that critical thinking has two distinct components which impact on personal and professional development. We have seen that Scriven and Paul (1987) show that critical thinking involves 'processing' skills which drive the gathering of information (research activities). In Chapter 3 Victoria Cooper outlines how the beliefs, values and principles of the practitioner also inform the choices and decisions regarding the conduct and process of investigation. Secondly, Webster-Wright (2009) shows critical thinking as a 'habit' of early childhood professional and intellectual commitment to guide behaviour and improve outcomes for practice. For example, Facione considered:

The ideal critical thinker is habitually inquisitive, well-informed, trustful of reason, open-minded, flexible, fair-minded in evaluation, honest in facing personal biases, prudent in making judgments, willing to reconsider and persistent in seeking results which are as precise as the subject and the circumstances of inquiry permit. (1990: 3)

Stupnisky et al. (2007) extend the notion of habit to that of a 'disposition' which Pascarella and Terenzini (2005) regard as a willingness to apply critical thinking skills. Perhaps when dealing with young children and their families another disposition could be added to Facione's list. The investigation featured in Chapter 3 (Ellis, 2007 unpublished) shows that Carole possesses many of Facione's traits but also demonstrates empathy with the people and situation she meets. The following short statements illustrate that she possesses the qualities for critical thinking. Can you spot them?

I hope that my views, values and initial assumptions will not impose on my research, it is my intention to reflect continually on my thoughts, findings and bias so that I reach a true understanding of the outcomes and at all times give attention to the ethical considerations.

I work in an area of 350 square miles; my role requires me to support families while recognising the value and dignity of each child and parent using our service. I work alone in referred families' home environments; I need to identify the needs of the community and provide sessions from the relevant children's centres that families can access. In order to do this effectively it is necessary for me to have knowledge and understanding about the needs of the communities that I work amongst and I am aware that this means I have to build relationships with the families in order to find out what is needed.

... The Childcare Act (DES, 2006a) requires local authorities to work together to identify parents and prospective parents who are unlikely to use early child-hood services – fathers are particularly mentioned. Reflection on how I was going to achieve this led me to approach the midwife who runs ante-natal classes from the Children's Centre. (Adapted from Ellis, 2007 unpublished)

Carole's experience can also be aligned to Moon's (2004) outline of dialogic reflection and the essence of positioning theory (Tirado and Galvez, 2007). This involves reasoning, and takes into account the broader contexts for practice. That is, it involves conscious engagement with historical, social and political contexts noted in other sections of this text, so that discussion of the outcomes considers the environment outside the particular setting. In other words, if you undertake your investigation as a supervisor in an infant/toddler room, your work needs to be informed by an investigation and consideration of the external features of policy that impact on your practice – social justice and family welfare agendas for example.

To ensure a dialogic approach to reflection on the research process and outcomes, Denscombe (2010) shows it is possible to pose a number of questions about the process – as noted previously in Chapter 6.

What has it meant for those closely involved with the researcher?

Can what was found be compared and contrasted with the subject literature search or what others have done?

What was found and was it valuable?

How does what was found inform and impact upon practice?

Has the process changed the researcher?

Did the process change the research methods or the nature of the research itself?

These questions place the investigator in an internal dialogue covering personal, professional, setting and practitioner positioning to identify specific dimensions of change and link directly to the personal and reflective positioning points in Figure 7.1.

However, stepping back a little, we can also identify that the projects described in this book and those initiated in practice all originate from a small question or initial thought – how can I improve? Why? What happens if we ...? And so on. This small step, the posing of the first question, will set you on the process of change which is facilitated by work-based investigation, but which itself is strongly representative of the qualities for practice outlined by Maxine Greene (1995). Her view can be summarised by the contention that only practitioners engaged in a reflection and a journey of self-awareness can engage effectively with supporting less experienced others – be they children or colleagues. Similarly, Duff et al. explain that: 'Just as self-initiated activity is critical to the child's development, so are reflection, self-evaluation, and self-direction critical to the process of professional development' (1995: 83). Or, in Clouder's view: '... reflective practice involves the critical analysis of everyday working practices to improve competence and promote professional development' (2000: 211). Tracy's study, based on the use of ICT in her setting, is evidence of Clouder's view as during her conclusion she states:

> Looking back at what I have completed over the past six months, I am amazed. When I started this project I felt that I couldn't see the end and didn't know which direction to turn. I'm glad I picked this topic to look at, because it has shown me that my views and beliefs were correct and [this] has given me the confidence to push the use of ICT within my setting more. As a result, I have been given the responsibility of implementing ICT to Key Stage 1, and have one afternoon a week to teach the children ICT skills. (Davies, 2007 unpublished: 10)

In other words, new professional positioning is an outcome of research, and reflection is crucial to the enhancement of professional management and leadership of teams. Bubb and Earley (2007) show that effective leadership is dependent on practitioners who will facilitate research-engaged and research-informed teams.

Changing a personal position through a questioning approach

As we saw in Chapter 1, Sue Foster's reflection as a nursery owner/ manager on her investigation into developing reflective practice in the setting (Foster, 2008 unpublished) involved an outcome which centred on self-awareness first rather than the features of her practice and her colleagues in the team, which had been the main focus of her investigation. The outcome of this critical reflection meant that development or improvement in reflective practice and the ability of others to engage with this first required a change in the values and assumptions of *herself* as the leader – a new personal 'position' as the result of appraising her values and attitudes as shown in Figure 7.1. Sue writes:

> I realise that my expectations must have weighed very heavily on my staff. The targets I had in mind at the outset have now become a longer journey. However, I do feel that we took the first steps towards that goal.
>
> The process was an education for me. I believe I am now better equipped to lead my staff team as I have gained a better understanding of reflection, the barriers to it, how to facilitate adult learning and what my individual practitioners need from me as a role model and leader. At times I lost sight of their individuality, needs and abilities. I need to find ways of becoming more empathic and of developing a culture more conducive to adult learning. I began the project from a rather lofty position as the person with the answers.
>
> My research proved my own theory that reflective practice is a risky business which can put you in a vulnerable position! It was uncomfortable to realise that the lack of reflection in my staff team was as much about me as it was about them. I have since begun a 'Leader in Me' (Covey, 2008) project where each member of staff has chosen an area of practice to investigate and develop however they choose. I have been surprised at how, given complete freedom, they have taken on the challenge and shown considerable reflective practice. (Adapted from Foster, 2008 unpublished)

Much has been written on reflective practice and useful texts are indicated in the suggested reading at the end of the chapter. For the most part, critical reflective practice is characterised by a willingness to *question* in order to affect and assess change. So far, we have highlighted personal change as an impact of research investigation and internal reflection. Consciousness of a wider context also enables an examination of the social and cultural factors influencing our personal position. For example, it was necessary for Sue to question all aspects contributing to her findings and identify which she was able to change. In the example above, and as outlined in Chapter 1, the change action resulting from questioning is a changed personal position in terms of the power dynamic in the team and the setting – resulting in a more collaborative approach to practice and engaging the creative thinking and reflection of others.

For student practitioners involved with formal reporting, the framework of questions provides a strategy for demonstrating personal critical thinking. It is possible to use Figure 7.1 to interrogate the impact of research in terms of each element of the personal dimension in order to demonstrate a new position. Thus what is the impact on:

- motivation and values;

- ethical understanding and practice;

- engagement with theory/discourse;

- ability to contribute to knowledge construction;

- ability to gather and manage 'data' as outcomes from investigation;

- ability to engage in collaborative working; and

- abilities/qualities to lead practice.

Examples of outcomes for experienced practitioners – as changes in personal and professional positioning – are illustrated in the following section. You are encouraged to make conscious links back to these points and Figure 7.1 while reading these reflections.

Professional repositioning – impact on colleagues, children and families

Fleet and Patterson (2001) consider early childhood practitioners are empowered learners who build their working knowledge through spirals of engagement over time. We have already seen that, just as water ripples outwards when a pebble is dropped into it, so Tracy's (Davies, 2007 unpublished) and Sue's (Foster, 2008 unpublished) research had an impact in their 'settings' as the ripples spread outwards, affecting colleagues, curriculum delivery and the children – a sound example of the holistic characteristics of the sector identified in Fleet and Patterson's work. The following paragraphs look at other examples of personal and professional change and how they represent this ripple effect.

As an accredited childminder and community pre-school leader, Alison (Jackson, 2008 unpublished) was interested to critically investigate perspectives on quality within her settings. In particular, she had begun to personally question the accepted discourse on quality as a purely practical construct, which she felt was not focused on the experience of children and families. Ali's study is fully outlined in Reed and Canning (2010). For our purposes, the significant impact of the investigation was her development as a professional in the sector – in particular her position in terms of national discourse. She was certainly surprised that a Foundation Degree investigation should contribute to an academic publication as an example of critical reflection, but she also writes of the confidence the process gave her to express her views in local authority networks and committees, to challenge 'expert' opinion and to contribute to the local discourse about what constitutes 'good practice'. Ali's example is critical for the understanding of the potential professional repositioning resulting from small-scale investigation. She is shown to have 'moved' from the periphery of a community of practice, to an active change agent within it and is characteristic of the 'new' professionals discussed in Callan (2010).

Ali Jackson's work had beneficial outcomes in terms of improved engagement with parents as partners for supporting children's learning and development. In a different study, Liz (Olliver, 2008 unpublished) as deputy nursery manager looked at the home-school diary system and the process of communication within her setting. Here Liz reflects on the change she went through as a professional following the completion of her research – particularly in understanding the wider 'discourse'.

> This whole topic of communication gave [me] a greater understanding of [my] work, as well as that of other practitioners within the setting. It was evident that practice must relate to theory and current literature, as well as government legislation as they are all intertwined and form a reflective cycle. The research itself was affected by time constraints and work commitments, yet it is apparent that research, in order to be completely current, must evolve in that way. (Olliver, 2008 unpublished: 24)

The research findings were used to inform staff, improve practice in the setting and encourage better communication with parents. Home-school diaries had attracted little response from parents, making the practitioners think their time was better spent with the children rather than writing copious notes in a diary which did not seem to develop 'communication' but simply 'inform'. Other researchers may have agreed with the conclusions of the team and withdrawn the diary system – however, following critical reflection on all factors, Liz

> recommended a full staff meeting to discuss the nursery diaries and the impact they have on the practitioner's daily routine. This would conclude in the involvement of the parents within the setting who may be given the opportunity to 'opt out' of the Nursery diary practice, or if they wished to continue, they must make a greater contribution by replying to the practitioner's previous comments, or at the very least, sign to acknowledge their last entry. (Olliver, 2008 unpublished: 24)

The investigation of parent experience of all communication strategies utilised by the setting revealed a high degree of satisfaction overall. This small change in shared understanding of the purpose and management of the diary system resulted in a more realistic use of the diaries as one aspect of this broader strategy and did much to promote positive relationships between practitioners and families. Involving her colleagues in analysing the diary system and including parents in the dissemination of her research findings helped initiate a change in the community of the setting, while the literature review helped the team leaders understand the need for an efficient and beneficial communication method between parents and staff. The benefit to the children of this enhanced mutual understanding between the adults involved in supporting the curriculum should be clearly apparent and Liz linked this improvement to the (English) EYFS requirements (DCSF, 2008a) when writing her report for the Foundation Degree assessment.

Summary

If, as the result of research, an improvement in practice and/or an improvement in a practitioner's understanding of what they are doing occur, then the investigation can be shown to have been 'useful'. This chapter has provided strategies through which inexperienced researchers can fully demonstrate their learning in terms of personal and professional impact. Research carried out by practitioners covers a broad spectrum of research 'types' and levels of formality. It also leads to change which involves technical local adaptations and improvement to the implementation of national frameworks for practice. Personal changes occur as the researcher undergoes a change to their way of thinking or knowing due to the insights they have acquired through investigation. Each represents a new 'position'. Liz, Tracy, Carol, Alison and Sue clearly display personal change as they 'think out loud' in their dissertations to help the reader understand the development of their thinking and learning. Each noticed and questioned an aspect of practice, worked on it and each developed from this experience in terms of professional roles. However, it is also apparent that it was not only the researchers who benefited from the research in terms of the communities involved. All the practitioners featured in this chapter model the importance of 'insider' research which engages collaboratively with children and families – in this way, demonstrating the knowledge, skills, participative attributes and personal qualities required of leaders in the sector, and more significantly, demonstrating the ability to contribute to national discussion and discourse on the future of the sector such as suggested by Moss (2010). Each is continuing a learning journey through ongoing professional development.

Further reading

The following texts each develop the key themes represented in this chapter from an applied perspective, a theoretical perspective and a critical perspective. They are useful sources for anyone wishing to develop the depth of their understanding of this area of practice.

Moon, J. (2004) *A Handbook of Reflective and Experiential Learning: Theory and Practice*. Oxford: RoutledgeFalmer.

Reed, M. and Canning, N. (eds) (2011) *Reflective Practice in the Early Years*. London: Sage.

Webster-Wright, A. (2009) 'Reframing professional development through understanding authentic professional learning', *Review of Educational Research*, 79 (2): 702–39.

Planning, undertaking and disseminating research in early childhood settings: an ethical framework[1]

Joy Cullen, Helen Hedges and Jane Bone

Chapter overview

Sue Callan and Michael Reed

At the start of this book, we explained how this chapter underlines a process we (as editors) went through while constructing the text. We sought out knowledge about research in practice and this meant looking at the world though different lenses, especially the world of the practitioner. This necessitated an exploration of the work of other researchers and an attempt to understand their position as researchers and writers. As a result, we considered the ongoing work of colleagues in New Zealand and, when reading the particular paper that forms this chapter, we felt its message informed and challenged aspects of research in practice. This is because the authors consider not only the component parts of an ethical framework, but place this within the context of early childhood. We felt this approach supported our own values and beliefs and added weight to the view expressed by Carla Solvason in Chapter 2 where she encourages us to consider purpose and ethicality as primary components of researching practice. The authors' approach should be seen as informing practice and researching practice at a number of levels: firstly, as a useful and accessible ethical framework which will be of value to policy-makers and those who lead practice, as well as practitioners who engage in practice-based evaluation. Additionally, it will be of value to university and college tutors and local authority development workers, who all have to provide clear ethical guidance to those who engage in research. Importantly, it transcends professional disciplines and recognises the importance of children and families who allow us the privilege of entering their world. It also provides – for those who support the professional development of others – a framework for discussion and reflection: not only on the functional aspects of ethical practice, but its purpose and impact on the children we all strive to protect. We also felt it offered a framework which can be used in early years settings to examine and refine policies and practices about the ethical position expected of insider and outsider researchers. When you read it, you will realise it was written for an audience that resides in New Zealand. Where appropriate, in conjunction with the original authors, we have modified the framework to make it accessible to a UK audience. Importantly, its inclusion tells us that research does lead to a sharing of views and findings and that we can all learn from each other. We have retained the authors' suggested reading list within this chapter as it will undoubtedly inform and support practice as well as practitioner investigations.

An ethical framework[2]

In recent years there has been an increase in research activities in the early childhood community in New Zealand. Lecturers in academic positions have been upgrading to doctoral qualifications. Early childhood teachers are proceeding to postgraduate studies and carrying out research to meet postgraduate requirements. (This process mirrors developments in the UK.) The concept of action research has entered professional discourse.

Teachers may also be asked to participate in a range of outside research projects funded by the Ministry of Education as part of its early childhood initiatives and academic research led by tertiary partners. The annual New Zealand Early Childhood Research Symposia and the range of articles in *New Zealand Research in Early Childhood Education* reflect the rapid growth of the early childhood research culture. Whether as participant or researcher, an awareness of ethical considerations should guide responsible decision-making about research activities. The growth of qualitative research, in particular, has challenged researchers to acknowledge the ethical tensions that permeate the research process. Participation in formal ethics review procedures does not negate the researcher's responsibility to engage in ongoing ethical decision-making.

This framework focuses on ethical dilemmas and issues specifically related to research in early childhood settings. It should be read in conjunction with the guidelines and codes of ethics for researchers developed by universities, research associations and other organisations that take account of the responsibilities of researchers and provide some protection for participants by ensuring a process of ethical clearance. These reflect ethical principles such as:

- respect for persons;

- minimisation of harm and maximisation of benefits;

- informed consent;

- voluntary participation;

- respect for privacy and confidentiality (or credit where appropriate);

- avoidance of unnecessary deception;

- avoidance of conflict of interest;

- Te Tiriti o Waitangi considerations (a long-standing treaty established so that indigenous peoples have rights that are respected and developed within the whole community; the Treaty upholds the principle of partnership between Māori and the Crown);

- social and cultural sensitivity;

- justice.

The framework applies to research that may be conceptualised on a continuum from 'insider' teacher and early years practitioner research to 'outsider' university/contract research. Ethical considerations related to teacher reflective practice and self-review may overlap with this statement, although specific examples of these activities are not included. Ethical decision-making can be guided by two perspectives: universal ethical principles and a focus on relationships. Ethical principles underpin the issues and considerations outlined in the framework. The framework also reflects a focus on the relationships involved in a research setting. A relationships perspective is particularly important for small-scale qualitative studies in a single setting, and when action research and other methodologies involve researchers and participants in more than one role. The framework is structured according to the processes of planning, undertaking and disseminating research and poses issues for:

- teachers and practitioners intending to carry out research as part of their professional role, for postgraduate research requirements or as participants in government-funded projects;

- teachers and practitioners who have been asked to participate in research by colleagues;

- teachers who have been asked to participate in research by outsider researchers (e.g. academic researchers, postgraduate researchers, contract researchers); and

- outsider researchers who wish to approach early years settings to participate in research.

Each of the three parts (planning, undertaking, disseminating) is based on issues relating to the unique aspects of working in early childhood settings, that is researching with young children, researching in a team environment and relationships with parents, families, and communities. General requirements that arise from the ethical principles above, for example for informed consent, are not covered as these are covered in generic codes of ethics for researchers.

Part A. Planning the proposed research: research questions, design and procedures

1. Researching with young children

Questions

- Are the research topic and questions appropriate for the age group?

- Are the data gathering procedures appropriate for the age group?

- Are the children able to give consent/assent?

- Do the procedures make good use of children's time?

- Who benefits from the research?

- Has the outsider researcher considered the time involved in building a relationship with the children to ensure authentic findings?

- How will non-participant children be excluded from records/data (e.g. field notes, photographs, videos, audiotapes – see also informed consent about the use of photographs (see this subject in 3 below)?

- Have Māori (indigenous) communities and other cultural groups been consulted about the appropriateness of the research topic for their children?

Considerations
Particular research topics may be quite inappropriate to research with young children and/or particular cultural groups. Some research plans that involve children in activities that are age inappropriate or that might damage self-esteem need to be reconsidered. Researchers must be sensitive to the needs of the children, e.g. privacy, fatigue, interests, safety, and acknowledge that the research may not always be the priority for these reasons. Teacher researchers and outsider researchers should plan ahead for their response to such situations and be aware of the non-verbal and verbal means through which children may 'withdraw consent'.

2. Researching in a team environment

Questions

- Do all staff need to agree to participate? Is the research feasible if one staff member does not want to participate?

- Is voluntary participation of staff constrained by a power relationship (e.g. head teacher–colleague)?

- Does the involvement of one staff member impinge on the roles and responsibilities of others?

- Is the research or presence of a researcher likely to change team roles or team dynamics?

- Will the research be affected if a member of staff changes during the course of the research?

- Is the research focus appropriate (e.g. appraisals and self-review)?

- How much personal time will teachers be expected to contribute to research activities?

Considerations
All research activity must be good use of teachers' time and have benefits for the early years setting. Team roles and dynamics should be considered when agreeing to participate in both teacher research and outsider research. In a team environment individual participation may have unexpected outcomes for the whole team, and subsequently the setting's programme and children. Potential conflicts of interest between teacher roles and researcher roles should be identified.

3. Relationships with parents, families and communities

Questions

- Are there cultural beliefs and practices that affect access decisions and processes?

- Do parents/caregivers understand the full implications of the research questions and processes?

- Do parents/caregivers understand the distinction between the research and the setting's normal teaching programme?

- Are informed consent procedures in place for each specific research project, or part of the project? (In both New Zealand and the United Kingdom the use of photographs of children and the distribution of photographs would be subject to a rigorous process of obtaining consent. Outsider researchers obtain formal ethical clearance through tertiary institutions or through other accredited ethics committees.)

- Have parents/families been informed about storage of data?

Considerations
Generic approval from parents/guardians to observe children does not exempt researchers, including teacher researchers, from the use of specific informed consent procedures for research projects. Informed consent procedures should consider cultural beliefs and practices and may require prior consultation within the community/ies.

Part B. Research processes: undertaking the research

1. Researching with young children

Questions

- Is there ongoing negotiation and sensitivity with regard to consent/ assent and voluntary participation?

- Is the researcher sensitive to the reality of the everyday teaching and learning processes?

- What is the effect of the research (e.g. time taken) on the teaching and learning environment?

- Are the data gathering techniques working as planned? Do they need modification to account for young children's participation?

- What happens in the research when original participants leave and new children join the group?

Considerations
Wherever possible, researchers should ensure that research activities do not disrupt children's routines or play. Moreover, when young children are involved the research activity may not be top priority. Researchers must be prepared to intervene in situations where children's well-being is compromised. Researchers must be sensitive to the needs of the children, for example, privacy, fatigue, interests. Researchers must be aware that children may be trying to please the researcher by remaining involved and be alert to differing participation levels from day to day. Consider that children may be 'withdrawing consent' through non-verbal as well as verbal means. If the approved research activity is additional to the normal environment, the amount of time children are involved in the research must be monitored. Teacher researchers must be aware of a potential conflict of interest in their dual roles.

2. Researching in a team environment

Questions

- Is there ongoing negotiation and sensitivity with regard to consent and voluntary participation?

- Is the ability to withdraw from the research until a particular point clear?

- Who will monitor and take responsibility for any changes that occur in team dynamics?

- What is the effect of the research (e.g. time taken) on the teaching and learning environment?

- Does the researcher have a responsibility if s/he observes unacceptable practices?

- What happens if the researcher/s change during the time span of the research?

Considerations
A first consideration is to distinguish the use of reflective practice for evaluative/teaching purposes compared with research purposes. Reflective practice/enquiry/research are likely to be on a continuum of activity, each with their own ethical considerations. There is potential conflict of interest when the researcher is a teacher in the early years setting. Colleagues may feel pressured to continue with the research even when they are uncomfortable with changes in team dynamics or the effect of the research on the learning and teaching environment.

3. Relationships with parents, families and communities

Questions

- Where outsider researchers are involved, what role do teachers have in enlisting participants?

- Is there ongoing negotiation and sensitivity with regard to consent and voluntary participation?

- Is the ability to withdraw from the research until a particular point clear?

- Are parents/families/communities informed or negotiated with when research questions and processes are modified?

- How are new parents and families that join the setting informed about the research? Do they feel pressured to join existing projects?

Considerations
Researchers must consider ways that parents, families and communities can be involved in ongoing and legitimate decision-making with regard

to research participation and research processes. In addition, there may be stages of consent applied in a long-term project. The researcher has ultimate responsibility for research processes and should not put undue pressures on parents and families who may have other priorities.

Part C. Disseminating data and findings

1. Researching with young children

Questions

- How will visual data such as photographs and videos be used in presentations and publications? Are there issues of anonymity/confidentiality? Is the use of visual data fair and equitable for all participants?

- Has consent been negotiated for visual data to be used in PowerPoint presentations and lectures?

- Are parents aware of the ethical issues in consent procedures regarding the use of visual data?

- Is there a time limit on the use of visual data?

- Can parents assist researchers by reading transcripts to children or discussing other data with them as validation processes?

Considerations
Researchers need to consider ways that children can be empowered to participate in validation and dissemination processes. Researchers have a responsibility to ensure that children are not reduced to 'cuteness' in the dissemination of research findings. As participants in the research process, children have the same rights as adults who are involved in the research. Photographs and video footage should be carefully stored and not included in copies of presentation material given to conference or seminar participants.

2. Researching in a team environment

Questions

- Can the teaching team use outsider researcher/s' data for other purposes? Has this been negotiated?

- Whose knowledge is valued in presentations and publications?

- Can researcher and teacher interpretations coexist?

- What procedures will be used to validate findings?

- What happens if teachers and others in the setting disagree with a researcher's findings?

- What will happen if there are negative implications/findings?

Considerations
Researchers and teachers need to have thought through the use of data for curriculum documentation, any other documentation, spin-off projects and such like. Researchers have an obligation to be transparent in the ways that they interpret, validate and disseminate research. They also have a responsibility to ensure that participants are supported to act on findings.

3. Relationships with parents, families and communities

Questions

- How will parents/families/communities be informed about the results and findings of a study?

- Have procedures for sharing data (e.g. videos) with parents/families been considered?

- Can a second round of consent processes be used to approve the use of visual data in presentations and publications?

- Whose knowledge is valued in presentations and publications?

- What will happen if there are negative implications/findings?

Considerations
Researchers have an obligation to be transparent in the ways that they interpret, validate and disseminate research. In particular, researchers must consider ways that parents, families and communities can be involved in ongoing and legitimate decision-making with regard to research dissemination.

Part D. Some general concerns

1. Mentoring and research
Research mentors need to have a clear contractual arrangement with teachers and practitioners. Questions to ask include:

- Who is responsible for finding time and funding for the research?

- Who has control over the research?

- Whose responsibility is it to obtain ethical clearance and from whose organisation?

- Given the considerations in the above framework, when does a mentor step in when s/he perceives problems exist?

2. Conflicts of interest
Early childhood teachers and researchers often work within small communities and may have multiple roles (e.g. teacher, parent, post-graduate student, academic researcher, member of community/professional groups, student or associate teacher) that could impact on the research. Questions to ask include:

- Do subtle pressures to participate arise from the close networks in early childhood education?

- Do access procedures allow time for potential participants to independently consider the project and its implications for all participants?

3. Postgraduate research
Postgraduate researchers may need to meet institutional research requirements that may not be required by the participating settings. Questions to ask include:

- Have all interested bodies/people been consulted for access prior to approaching participants (e.g. management and/or relevant association or other umbrella body)?

- Have all institutional requirements been explained, including the requirement to inform ethics committees of any changes to procedures, following initial approval procedures?

- Do participants understand that they may perceive an academic report to be negative or threatening if issues are raised by researchers? Theses and academic publications require an analytical style that could be seen to criticise participants and settings.

- Who holds ownership of the data? Employers and tertiary institutions may have their own rights to ownership.

Summary

Undertaking research with human participants and especially with young children is a privilege. Ethical issues permeate all aspects of qualitative research and require close attention to decision-making about research topics and choices of methodologies, methods and dissemination of findings. Researchers have a responsibility to act in the best interests of their participants. This framework aims to focus those researching in early childhood settings on ethical principles and processes to consider throughout the research activities that involve children, teachers, parents, families and communities.

Notes

1. Reproduced with the kind permission of the journal *New Zealand Research in Early Childhood Education*, vol. 12 (2009).
2. An earlier version of this framework was published online at: http://www.childforum.com.

Ethical guidelines that complement this framework

Anae, M., Coxon, E., Mara, D., Wendt-Samu, T. and Finau, C. (2001) *Pasifika Research Guidelines*. Wellington: Ministry of Education. Online at: http://www.educationcounts.govt.nz/publications/pasifika_education/5915 (retrieved 21 April 2009).

Health Research Council (2008) *Guidelines for Researchers on Health Research Involving Maori*. Auckland: Health Research Council. Online at: http://www.hrc.govt.nz/assets/pdfs/publications/MHGuidelines%202008%20FINAL.pdf (retrieved 21 April 2009).

New Zealand Association for Research in Education (1998) *Ethical Guidelines*. Online at: http://www.nzare.org.nz/pdfs/NZARE_ethical guidelines.pdf (retrieved 21 April 2009).

Further reading

Bishop, R. (2005) 'Freeing ourselves from neocolonial domination in research: a Kaupapa Māori approach to creating knowledge', in N. K. Denzin and Y. Lincoln (eds), *Handbook of Qualitative Research*, 3rd edn. New York: Sage, pp. 109–38.

Discusses researcher power and positioning in relationships with Māori participants. Provides critical questions for researchers to consider before and during research activity related to five issues of power.

Bishop, R. and Glynn, T. (1999) *Culture Counts: Changing Power Relations in Education*. Palmerston North: Dunmore Press.
This book has an important focus on the Māori concept of *whanaungatanga* (relationships), particularly Chapter 3 addressing power and control issues in educational research.

Bone, J. (2005) 'Theorising in progress: an ethical journey: rights, relationships and reflexivity', *Australian Journal of Early Childhood*, 30 (1): 1–5.
A researcher reflects about challenges to ethical procedures, from children and adults in three different early childhood settings.

Coady, M. M. (2001) 'Ethics in early childhood research', in G. MacNaughton, S. A. Rolfe and I. Siraj-Blatchford (eds), *Doing Early Childhood Research: International Perspectives on Theory and Practice*. Buckingham: Open University Press, pp. 64–72.
A clear introduction to ethical aspects of research.

Cullen, J. (2005) 'The ethics of research in educational settings', in P. Adams, K. Vossler and C. Scrivens (eds), *Teachers' Work in Aotearoa New Zealand*. Southbank: Thomson Dunmore Press, pp. 252–61.
Discusses two perspectives on ethics – principlist and relationships – and the outsider–insider continuum of research.

Danby, S. and Farrell, A. (2005) 'Opening the research conversation', in A. Farrell (ed.), *Ethical Research with Children*. Maidenhead: Open University Press, pp. 49–67.
Focuses on children having the right to be fully informed about research. Discusses using evidence from research conversations with children about the process of having given consent to participate. Includes an example of a consent form.

Degotardi, S. (2008) 'Looking out and looking in: reflecting on conducting educational research in a child-care nursery', *The First Years: New Zealand Journal of Infant and Toddler Education*, 10 (2): 15–19.
Discusses tensions that arise in an observational research project in a long day-care nursery, extending ethics discussion into research with infants.

Dockett, S. and Perry, B. (2007) 'Trusting children's accounts in research', *Journal of Early Childhood Research*, 5 (1): 47–63.
Examines ethical principles and processes using two studies involving children in the context of Queensland, Australia. Highlights the complexity of ethical issues and the commitment required of researchers to ascertain, analyse and report children's perspectives.

Flewitt, R. (2005) 'Conducting research with young children: some ethical considerations', *Early Child Development and Care*, 175 (6): 553–65.
Reflexive account of ethnographic study of four three-year-old children in home and centre settings, particularly in relation to informed consent and use of visual data.

Goldstein, L. S. (2000) 'Ethical dilemmas in designing collaborative research: lessons learned the hard way', *International Journal of Qualitative Studies in Education*, 73 (5): 517–32.
An honest appraisal of the ethical dilemmas encountered by a university researcher when researching collaboratively with a classroom teacher.

Goodfellow, J. and Hedges, H. (2007) 'Early childhood practitioner research "centre stage": contexts, contributions and challenges', in L. Keesing-Styles and H. Hedges (eds), *Theorising Early Childhood Practice: Emerging Dialogues*. Baulkham Hills, NSW: Pademelon Press, pp. 187–210.
Discusses continuum of practitioner enquiry and research, and associated methodological and ethical issues.

Greig, A., Taylor, J. and Mackay, T. (2007) *Doing Research with Children*, 2nd edn. London: Sage.
Chapter 8, 'Consultation and participation with children in research', is helpful for considering a range of appropriate methodological approaches in relation to children's participation. Chapter 9, 'Ethics of doing research with children', considers ethics broadly and provides a table of good practice guidelines with useful questions.

Guo, K. (2009) 'Embedding self, others, culture and ethics in intercultural research', *New Zealand Research in Early Childhood Education*, 12: 141–52.
Describes dilemmas experienced when attempting to marry institutional ethical principles and cultural sensitivities in an early childhood research setting.

Hedges, H. (2002) 'Beliefs and principles in practice: ethical research with child participants', *New Zealand Research in Early Childhood Education*, 5: 31–47.
Describes, examines and problematises efforts to empower four-year-old children's participation in research activity.

Hill, M. (2005) 'Ethical considerations in researching children's experiences', in S. Greene and D. Hogan (eds), *Researching Children's Experience: Approaches and Methods*. London: Sage, pp. 61–86.
Provides an overview of ethical principles and decision-making processes. Provides a table of ethical issues with useful questions for researchers to consider. Lists matters that ought to be included in participant information provided to children. Examines different types of confidentiality such as public, social network and third-party.

Meade, A. (ed.) (2006) *Riding the Waves: Innovation in Early Childhood Education*. Wellington: NZCER Press.
This collection includes thoughtful accounts of the research experiences of teacher researchers, including relationships between teachers and research associates. Refer also to *Catching the Waves* (2005) and *Cresting the Waves* (2007), in the Innovation in Early Childhood Education series of reports, for descriptions of the research.

Moss, J. (2008) *Researching Education: Visually Digitally Spatially*. Rotterdam: Sense.
A collection that addresses issues concerning research and ethics in a visual/digital world.

Podmore, V. (2006) *Observation: Origins and Approaches to Early Childhood Research and Practice*. Wellington: NZCER.
Considers ethics in relation to assessment and research methodologies and practices.

Stephenson, A. (2009) 'Horses in the sandpit: photography, prolonged involvement and "stepping back" as strategies for listening to children's voices', *Early Child Development and Care*, 779 (2): 131–41.
A thoughtful, reflexive account of methodological and ethical issues related to naturalistic observations and accessing children's understandings.

Tolich, M. (ed.) (2001) *Research Ethics in Aotearoa New Zealand*. Auckland: Pearson Education.
Contains commentaries from established New Zealand researchers on aspects of ethical research, including chapters on Māori research, interviewing children and families, classroom research.

References

Abbot, L. and Nutbrown, C. (2001) *Experiencing Reggio Emilia: Implications for Preschool Provision*. Buckingham: Open University Press.

Alderson, P. (2005) 'Designing ethical research with children', in A. Farrell (ed.), *Ethical Research with Children*. Maidenhead: Open University Press.

Alderson, P. and Morrow, V. (2011) *The Ethics of Research with Children and Young People: A Practical Handbook*. London: Sage.

Altrichter, H., Feldman, A., Posch, P. and Somekh, B. (2008) *Teachers Investigate Their Work: An Introduction to Action Research Across the Professions*, 2nd edn. London: Routledge.

Anning, A., Cullen, J. and Fleer, M. (2009) *Early Childhood Education, Society and Culture*, 2nd edn. London: Sage.

Appleby, K. (2010) 'Reflective thinking, reflective practice', in M. Reed and N. Canning (eds), *Reflective Practice in the Early Years*. London: Sage.

Armistead, J. (2008) 'A Study of Children's Perspectives on the Quality of Their Experiences in Early Years Provision'. PhD thesis, University of Northumbria at Newcastle, School of Health, Community and Education Studies. Online at: http://northumbria.openre-pository.com/.../10145/.../armistead.josephine_phd.pdf.

Atkinson, P. and Hammersley, M. (1994) 'Ethnography and participant observation', in N. K. Denzin and Y. S. Lincoln (eds), *Handbook of Qualitative Research*. Thousand Oaks, CA: Sage.

Aubrey, C., David, T., Godfrey, R. and Thompson, L. (2000) *Early Childhood Educational Research: Issues in Methodology and Ethics*. London: Routledge.

Baum, A. and McMurray-Schwarz, P. (2007) 'Research 101: Tools for reading and inter-preting early childhood research', *Early Childhood Education Journal*, 34 (6). Online at: http://www.springerlink.com/index/6322520228624476.pdf.

Blaxter, L., Hughes, C. and Tight, M. (2001) *How to Research*, 2nd edn. Buckingham: Open University Press.

Bogdan, R. C. and Biklen, S. K. (2006) *Qualitative Research in (Validation) and Qualitative (Inquiry) Studies: An Introduction to Theory and Methods*. London: Allyn & Bacon.

Bolton, G. (2005) *Reflective Practice: Writing and Professional Development*. London: Sage.

British Educational Research Association (BERA) (2004) *Revised Ethical Guidelines for Educational Research*. Online at: http://bera.ac.uk publications/guidelines.

Brookfield, S. (1995) *Becoming a Critically Reflective Teacher*. San Francisco: Jossey-Bass.

Bubb, S. and Earley, P. (2007) *Leading and Managing Continuing Professional Development*, 2nd edn. London: Paul Chapman.

Callan, S. (2007) 'The Foundation Degree in Early Years: Student Perception of Themselves as Learners and the Experiences that Have Contributed to This View. Can an Exploration of These Issues Enhance Reflective Practice?' Unpublished MA thesis, University of Worcester.

Callan, S. (2010) 'From experienced practitioner to reflective professional', in M. Reed and N. Canning (eds), *Reflective Practice in the Early Years*. London: Sage.

Callan, S. and Morrall, A. (2009) 'Working with parents', in A. Robins and S. Callan (eds), *Managing Early Years Settings*. London: Sage.

Callan, S., Reed, M. and Smith, S. (2010) *Co-constructing Pedagogy for the Children's Workforce: Teaching and Learning in Academic Routes towards a 'New Professionalism'*. Paper presented at the conference Early Childhood Curriculum, Policy and Pedagogy in the 21st Century: An International Debate, Anglia Ruskin University.

Candy, L. (2006) *Practice Based Research: A Guide*, CCS Report: 2006-V1.0 November. Sydney: Creativity and Cognition Studios, University of Technology. Online at: http://www.creativityandcognition.com/resources/PBR%20Guide-l.l-2006.pdf.

Canning, N. (2009) 'Empowering communities through inspirational leadership', in A. Robins and S. Callan (eds), *Managing Early Years Settings*. London: Sage.

Canning, N. and Callan, S. (2010) 'Heutagogy – spirals of reflection to empower learners in higher education', *Reflective Practice: International and Multidisciplinary Perspectives*, 11 (1): 71–82.

Carr, M. and May, H. (2000) 'Te Whariki curriculum voices', in H. Penn (ed.), *Early Childhood Services: Theory, Policy and Practice*. Buckingham: Open University Press.

Carr, W. (2000) 'Partisanship in educational research', *Oxford Review of Education*, 26 (3/4): 495–501.

Cheng, L. (2005) *Changing Language Teaching Through Language Testing: A Washback Study*. Cambridge: Cambridge University Press.

Children's Workforce Development Council (CDWC) (2009) *Early Years Professional Status*. Leeds: CWDC.

Children's Workforce Development Council (CWDC) (2010) *Common Core Skills and Knowledge for the Children's Workforce*. Leeds: CWDC.

Christensen, P. and Prout, A. (2005) 'Anthropological and sociological perspectives on the study of children', in S. Greene and D. Hogan (eds), *Researching Children's Experience: Approaches and Methods*. Thousand Oaks, CA: Sage.

Clark, A. (2004) 'The Mosaic approach and research with young children', in *The Reality of Research with Children and Young People*. London: Sage.

Clark, A. and Moss, P. (2001) *Listening to Young Children: The Mosaic Approach*. London: National Children's Bureau.

Claxton, G. (1997) *Hare Brain, Tortoise Mind*. London: Fourth Estate.

Claxton, G. (2003) *The Intuitive Practitioner: On the Value of Not Always Knowing What One Is Doing*. Maidenhead: Open University Press.

Clouder, L. (2000) 'Reflective practice in physiotherapy', *Studies in Higher Education*, 25 (2): 211–23.

Clough, P. and Nutbrown, C. (2002) *A Student's Guide to Methodology: Justifying Enquiry*. London: Sage.

Clough, P. and Nutbrown, C. (2007) *A Student's Guide to Methodology: Justifying Enquiry*, 2nd edn. London: Sage.

Cohen, L. and Manion, L. (2000) *Research Methods in Education*, 5th edn. London: Routledge.

Cooke, G. and Lawton, K. (2008) *For Love or Money: Pay, Progression and Professionalization in the Early Years Workforce*. London: Institute for Public Policy Research.

Cooper, V. L. (2010) 'Distance learning and professional development', in M. Reed and N. Canning (eds), *Reflective Practice in the Early Years*. London: Sage.

Costley, C. and Armsby, P. (2007) 'Methodologies for undergraduates doing practitioner investigations at work', *Journal of Workplace Learning*, 19 (3): 131–45.

Costley, C., Elliott, G. and Gibbs, P. (2010) *Doing Work-Based Research: Approaches to Enquiry for Insider Researchers*. London: Sage.

Covey, S. (2008) *The Leader in Me*. London: Simon & Schuster.

Cullen, J., Hedges, H. and Bone, J. (2009) 'Planning, undertaking and disseminating research in early childhood settings: an ethical framework', *New Zealand Research in Early Childhood Education*, 12: 109–18.

Danby, S. and Farrell, A. (2006) 'Exploring consent and participation', in A. Farrell (ed.), *Exploring Ethical Research with Children*. Milton Keynes: Open University Press.

Data Protection Act 1998. Online at: http//:www.opsi.gov.uk/acts/acts1998/ukpga_19980029_en_1.

Davies, T. (2007) 'Are Children Motivated, Enjoy and Stay on Task Longer If They Use Information Communication Technology in the Literacy Hour?' Unpublished Foundation Degree thesis in Early Years, University of Worcester.

Denscombe, M. (2010) *The Good Research Guide: For Small-Scale Social Research Projects*, 4th edn. Buckingham: Open University Press.

Denzin, N. K. (1970) *The Research Act in Sociology*. Chicago: Aldine.

Denzin, N. K. (2006) *Sociological Methods: A Sourcebook*. Chicago: Aldine Transaction.

Denzin, N. K. and Lincoln, Y. (eds) (2003) *The Landscape of Qualitative Research: Theories and Issues*, 2nd edn. London: Sage.

Department for Children, Schools and Families (DCSF) (2007) *Children's Plan*. Nottingham: DCSF.

Department for Children, Schools and Families (DCSF) (2008a) *Statutory Framework for the Early Years Foundation Stage*. Nottingham: DCSF.

Department for Children, Schools and Families (DCSF) (2008b) *National Strategies Early Years Series*. Nottingham: DCSF.

Department for Children, Schools and Families (DCSF) (2008c) *Social and Emotional Aspects of Development*. Nottingham: DCSF.

Department for Education and Employment (DfEE) (1989) *The National Curriculum*. London: DfEE.

Department for Education and Skills (DfES) (1998) *The National Literacy Strategy*. London: DfES.

Department for Education and Skills (DfES) (2002) *Birth to Three Matters: A Framework to Support Children in Their Earliest Years*. London: DfES.

Department for Education and Skills (DfES) (2004) *Every Child Matters: Change for Children*. Nottingham: DfES.

Department for Education and Skills (DfES) (2006a) *The Children's Centre Practice Guidance and Planning and Performance Management Guidance*. Nottingham: DfES.

Department for Education and Skills (DfES) (2006b) *Childcare Act*. London: HMSO.

Department for Education and Skills (DfES) (2007a) *Aiming High for Children: Supporting Families*. Nottingham: DfES.

Department for Education and Skills (DfES) (2007b) *Sure Start Children's Centres. Phase Three Planning and Delivery*. Nottingham: DfES.

Dochy, F., Gijbels, S., Segers, M. and Bossche, P. (2011) *Psychological Theories of Learning in the Workplace*. London: Routledge.

Dockett, S. and Perry, B. (2005) 'Children's drawings: experiences and expectations of school', *International Journal of Equity and Innovation in Early Childhood*, 3 (2): 77–89.

Dockett, S., Einarsdottir, J. and Perry, B. (2009) 'Researching with children: ethical tensions', *Early Childhood Research*, 7 (3): 283–98.

Dowling, M. (2003) *Young Children's Personal Social and Emotional Development*. London: Paul Chapman.

Drury, R. (2007) *Young Bi-lingual Learners at Home and at School: Researching Multi-Lingual Voices*. Stoke-on-Trent: Trentham Books.

Duff, R., Brown, E. and Van Scoy, I. (1995) 'Reflection and self-evaluation: keys to professional development', *Young Children*, 50 (4): 81–8.

Early Childhood Australia Inc. (2010) *The Code of Ethics*. Online at: http://www.early childhoodaustralia.org.au/code_of_ethics/early_childhood_australias_code_of__ ethics.html#top.

Ecclestone, K. (2005) 'Against over-emphasis on self-esteem and expectations in education', in D. Hayes (ed.), *RoutledgeFalmer Guide to Key Debates in Education*. London: RoutledgeFalmer.

Edwards, A. (2004) 'Education', in S. Fraser, V. Lewis, S. Ding, M. Kellett and C. Robinson (eds), *Doing Research with Children and Young People*. Milton Keynes: Open University Press.

Einarsdottir, J. (2005) 'Playschool in pictures: children's photographs as a research method', *Early Child Development and Care*, 175 (6): 523–41.

Einstein, Albert (undated) Online at: http://www.fys.ku.dk/~raben/einstein.

Eisner, E. (1993) 'Objectivity in educational research', in M. Hammersley (ed.), *Educational Research: Current Issues*. Milton Keynes: Open University Press.

Ellis, C. (2007) 'A Feasibility Study into the Enhancement of Paternal Engagement at a Fathers' Group in the Children's Centre'. Unpublished Foundation degree thesis in Early Years, University of Worcester.

Ennis, R. (1993) 'Critical thinking assessment', *Theory into Practice*, 32 (3): 179–86.

Eysenbach, G. and Till, J. E. (2001) 'Ethical issues in qualitative research on Internet communities', *British Medical Journal*, 323: 1103–5. Online at: http://www.bmj.com/ cgi/content/full/323/7321/1103.

Fabien, H. and Dunlop, A. L. (2002) 'Conclusions: debating transitions, continuity and progression', in H. Fabien and A. L. Dunlop (eds), *Transitions in the Early Years*. London: RoutledgeFalmer.

Facione, P. (1990) *Critical Thinking: A Statement of Expert Consensus for Purposes of Educational Assessment and Instruction: Research Findings and Recommendations*. Newark, NJ: American Philosophical Association.

Fay, B. (1996) *Contemporary Philosophy of Social Science: A Multi-cultural Approach*. Oxford: Blackwell Press.

Finlay, L. and Gough, B. (2003) *Reflexivity: A Practical Guide for Researchers in Health and Social Sciences*. Oxford: Blackwell.

Fleer, M. (2003) 'Early childhood education as an evolving "community of practice" or as lived "social reproduction": researching the "taken-for granted"', *Contemporary Issues in Early Childhood*, 4 (1): 64–79.

Fleet, A. and Patterson, C. (2001) Online at: http://ecrp.uiuc.edu/v3n2/fleet.html.

Flewitt, R. (2005) 'Conducting research with young children: some ethical considerations', *Early Child Development and Care*, 175 (6): 553–65.

Ford, N. (2011) *The Essential Guide to Using the Web for Research*. London: Sage.

Foster, S. (2006) 'Barriers to Good Practice for Outdoor Play'. Unpublished Foundation Degree thesis in Early Years, University of Worcester.

Foster, S. (2008) 'An Exploration of How to Promote Reflective Practice in Staff at My Setting'. Unpublished BA (Hons) thesis in Early Childhood Studies, University of Worcester.

Freire, P. (1973) *The Practice of Freedom*. Aylesbury: Hazell, Watson & Viney.

Fullan, M. (2001) *Leading in a Culture of Change*. San Fransisco: John Wiley.

Glaser, B. and Strauss, A. (1967) *The Discovery of Grounded Theory: Strategies for Qualitative Research*. Chicago: Aldine.

Goodfellow, J. (2007) 'Researching with/for whom? Stepping in and out of practitioner research', *Australian Journal of Early Childhood*, December.

Goodfellow, J. and Hedges, H. (2007) 'Practitioner research "centre stage": contexts, contributions and challenges', in L. Keesing-Styles and H. Hedges (eds), *Theorizing Early Childhood Practice: Emerging Dialogues*. Castle Hill, NSW: Pademelon Press.

Greene, M. (1995) *Releasing the Imagination: Essay on Education, the Arts and Social Change*. San Francisco: Jossey-Bass.

Hammersley, M. (ed.) (1993) *Educational Research: Current Issues*. Milton Keynes: Open University Press.

Hammersley, M. (2005) 'Countering the "new orthodoxy" in educational research: a response to Phil Hodkinson', *British Educational Research Journal*, 31 (2): 139–55.

Hammersley, M. (2009) 'Against the ethicists: on the evils of ethical regulation', 12 (3): 211–25.

Harris, A. (1998) 'Effective teaching: a review of the literature', *School Leadership and Management*, 18 (2): 169–83.

Hatten, R., Knapp, D. and Salonga, R. (1997) 'Action Research: Comparison with the Concepts of "The Reflective Practitioner" and "Quality Assurance"'. Online at: http://www.scu.edu.au/schools/gcm/ar/arr/arow/rdr.html.

Haviland, M., Johnson, K., Orr, L. and Lienert, T. (2005) 'Being an insider and/or outsider', *Stronger Families Learning Exchange*, Bulletin No. 7, Spring.

Hayes, A. (2001) 'Design issues', in G. MacNaughton, S. A. Rolfe and I. Siraj-Blatchford (eds), *Doing Early Childhood Research – International Perspectives on Theory and Practice*. Buckingham: Open University Press.

Hedges, H. (2001) 'Teacher/researchers in early childhood: ethical responsibilities to children', *Networks*, 4 (2): 1–8.

Hedges, H. and Cullen, J. (2005) 'Subject knowledge in early childhood curriculum and pedagogy: beliefs and practices', *Contemporary Issues in Early Childhood*, 6 (1): 66–79.

Heron, J. and Reason, P. (2001) 'The practice of co-operative inquiry: research with rather than on people', in P. Reason and H. Bradbury (eds), *Handbook of Action Research: Participative Inquiry and Practice*. London: Sage.

Hertz, R. (1997) *Reflexivity and Voice*. Thousand Oaks, CA: Sage.

Hitchcock, G. and Hughes, D. (1995) *Research and the Teacher: A Qualitative Introduction to School-Based Research*, 2nd edn. London: Routledge.

Hodkinson, P. (2004) 'Research as a form of work: expertise, community and methodological objectivity', *British Educational Research Journal*, 30 (1): 9–26.

Holliday, A. (2002) *Doing and Writing Qualitative Research*. London: Sage.

Holloway, W. and Jefferson, T. (2000) *Doing Qualitative Research Differently. Free Association, Narrative and the Interview Method*. London: Sage.

Jackson, A. (2008) 'How Do Parents and Carers Define and Measure Quality in Early Years Settings?' Unpublished Foundation Degree thesis in Early Years, University of Worcester.

Jackson, A. (2010) 'Defining and measuring quality in early years settings', in M. Reed and N. Canning (eds), *Reflective Practice in the Early Years*. London: Sage.

Janesick, V. J. (1994) 'The dance of qualitative research design', in N. Denzin and Y. Lincoln (eds), *Handbook of Qualitative Research*. Thousand Oaks, CA: Sage.

Janzen, M. (2008) 'Where is the (postmodern) child in early childhood education research?' *Early Years*, 28 (3): 287–98.

Kemmis, M. (2001) 'Exploring the relevance of critical theory for action research: emancipatory action research in the footsteps of Jürgen Habermas', in P. Reason and H. Bradbury (eds), *Handbook of Action Research*. Thousands Oaks, CA: Sage.

Le Gallais, T. (2003) *From Native to Stranger ... and Back Again? Questions for Reflective Practitioners*. Paper presented at the BERA Annual Conference, Herriott Watt University, Edinburgh.

Le Gallais, T. (2004) *Too Busy Reacting to Reflect! A Case Study of a Group of Novice Researchers Involved in their First Action Research Project Set Within an FE College in the West Midlands*. Paper presented at BERA Conference, UMIST, Online at: http://www. leeds.ac.uk/educol/documents/00003718.doc.

Lincoln, Y. S. (2010) 'What a long, strange trip it's been ... twenty-five years of qualitative and new paradigm research', *Qualitative Inquiry*, 16 (1): 3–9.

Lloyd, E. and Hallet, E. (2010a) 'Reconceptualising the early years profession in England: a comparison of policymaker and practitioner views', *Journal of Contemporary Issues in Early Childhood* (Australia), Spring.

Lloyd, E. and Hallet, E. (2010b) 'Professionalising the early childhood workforce in England: work in progress or missed opportunity', *Contemporary Issues in Early Childhood*, 11 (1): 75–88.

Lubeck, S. (1995) 'Nation as context: comparing child care systems across nations', *Teachers College Record*, 96 (3): 467–91.

McCart-Neilsen, J. (ed.) (1990) *Feminist Research Methods: Exemplary Readings in the Social Sciences*. London: Westview Press.

McNiff, J. and Whitehead, J. (2002) *Action Research Principles and Practice*. London: RoutledgeFalmer.

Malcolm, J. (1993) *Negotiating the Minefield: Practical and Political Issues in Policy Research*. University of Leeds, Conference Proceedings, Policy and Research.

Moon, J. (2004) *A Handbook of Reflective and Experiential Learning: Theory and Practice*. Oxford: Routledge.

Moss, P. (2003) *Beyond Caring: The Case for Reforming the Childcare and Early Years Workforce*. London: Day Care Trust/National Childcare Campaign.

Moss, P. (2010) 'We cannot continue as we are: the educator in an education for survival', *Contemporary Issues in Early Childhood*, 11 (1): 8–19.

Mukherji, P. and Albon, D. (2010) *Research Methods in Early Childhood: An Introductory Guide*. London: Sage.

New, R. S. (2008) 'Rethinking research in early care and education: joining Sally's quest', *Journal of Early Childhood Research*, 6 (1): 59–67.

Newman, L. and Pollnitz, L. (2002) 'Ethics in action: introducing the ethical response cycle', *Research in Practice*, 9 (3): 13–18.

O'Dochartaigh, N. (2002) *The Internet Research Handbook*. London: Sage.

O'Donoghue, T. and Punch, K. (2003) *Qualitative Educational Research in Action: Doing and Reflecting*. London: Routledge.

Oancea, A. (2005) 'Criticisms of educational research: key topics and levels of analysis', *British Educational Research Journal*, 31 (2): 157–83.

Oancea, A. and Pring, R. (2008) 'The importance of being thorough: on systematic accumulations of "what works" in education research', *Journal of Philosophy of Education*, 42 (15): 39–40.

Olliver, E. (2008) 'Communication with Parents – What Was Effective and Not Effective Within a Nursery School?' Unpublished Foundation Degree thesis in Early Years, University of Worcester.

Opie, C. (ed.) (2004) *Doing Educational Research*. London: Sage.

Osgood, J. (2006) 'Deconstructing professionalism in early childhood education: resisting the regulatory gaze', *Contemporary Issues in Early Childhood*, 7 (1). Online at: http://www.wwords.co.uk/pdf/freetoview.asp?j=ciec&vol=7&issue=1&year=2006&article=2Osgood_CIEC_7_1web.

Osgood, J. (2009) 'Childcare workforce reform in England and "the early years professional": a critical discourse analysis', *Journal of Education Policy*, 24 (6): 733–51.

Osgood, J. (2010) 'Multi-professionalism and the Early Years Professional: contested terrain', in R. Thompson (ed.), *Critical Practice in Work with Children and Young People*. Buckingham: Open University Press.

Pascarella, E. T. and Terenzini, P. T. (2005) *How College Affects Students: A Third Decade of Research*, Vol. 2. San Francisco: Jossey-Bass.

Patton, M. Q. (1987) *How to Use Qualitative Methods in Evaluation*. London: Sage.

Peim, N. (2009) 'Thinking resources for educational research methods and methodology', *International Journal of Research and Method in Education*, 32 (3): 235–48.

Philips, E. and Pugh, D. S. (1994) *How to Get a PhD*. London: Kogan Page.

Picken, L. (2007) 'Can the Reggio Emilia Approach Work Successfully Within the New Early Years Foundation Stage?' Unpublished Foundation Degree thesis in Early Years, University of Worcester.

Pilcher, M. (2009) 'Making a positive contribution', in A. Robins and S. Callan (eds), *Managing Early Years Settings*. London: Sage.

Plymouth Area Safeguarding Board (2010) 'Summary of Serious Case Review, Nursery "Z"'. Online at: http://www.plymouth.gov.uk/homepage/socialcareandhealtii/children ssocialcare/localsafeguardingchildrenboard/littletednurservreview.htm.

Powell, K., Danby, S. and Farrell, A. (2006) 'Investigating an account of children "passing notes" in the classroom: how boys and girls operate differently in relation to an everyday, classroom regulatory practice', *Journal of Early Childhood Research*, 4: 259–75.

Pugh, G. and Duffy, B. (2006) *Contemporary Issues in Early Years*, 4th edn. London: Sage.

Punch, M. (1994) 'Politics and ethics in qualitative research', in N. Denzin and Y. Lincoln (eds), *Handbook of Qualitative Research*. Thousand Oaks, CA: Sage.

Reed, M. (2011) 'Reflective practice and professional development', in A. Page-Smith and A. Craft (eds), *Developing Reflective Practice in the Early Years*, 2nd edn. Milton Keynes: Open University Press.

Reed, M. and Canning, N. (eds) (2010) *Reflective Practice in the Early Years*. London: Sage.

Reed, M. and Canning, N. (eds) (2011 in press) *Implementing Quality Improvement and Change in the Early Years*. London: Sage.

Reed, M. and Sansoyer, P. (2011 in press) 'Quality Improvement: integrated working', in M. Reed and N. Canning (eds), *Implementing Quality Improvement and Change in the Early Years*. London: Sage.

Rike, C. and Sharp, L. K. (2008) 'Assessing pre-service teachers' dispositions: a critical dimension of professional preparation', *Childhood Education*, 84 (3): 150–3.

Rinaldi, C. (2005) *In Dialogue with Reggio Emilia*. London: RoutledgeFalmer.

Roberts-Holmes, G. (2005) *Doing Your Early Years Research Project*. London: Paul Chapman.

Robins, A. and Callan, S. (2009) 'Mentoring and supporting teams', in A. Robins (ed.), *Managing Early Years Settings*. London: Sage.

Robins, A. and Callan, S. (eds) (2009) *Managing Early Years Settings*. London: Sage.

Robson, J. (2002) *Real World Research*, 2nd edn. Oxford: Blackwell.

Safford, K. and Hancock, R. (2010) 'Approaches to small-scale enquiry and research in schools', in K. Safford, M. Stacey and R. Hancock (eds), *Small-Scale Research in Primary Schools*. Berkshire: Open University Press.

Schiller, W. and Einarsdottir, J. (2009) 'Special issue: listening to young children's voices in research – changing perspectives/changing relationships', *Early Child Development and Care*, 179 (2): 125–30.

Schön, D. (1983) *The Reflective Practitioner: How Professionals Think in Action*. New York: Basic Books.

Schön, D. (1987) *Educating the Professional Practitioner*. San Fransico: Jossey-Bass.

Scriven, M. and Paul, R. (1987) 'Defining Critical Thinking: A Draft Statement for the National Council for Excellence in Critical Thinking'. Online at: http://www.criticalthinking.org/university/defining.html.

Smith, S. (2008) 'Foundation Degrees: Further Education or Highering Aspirations? To What Extent Do Further Education Institutions Support Transition into Higher Education?' Unpublished MA (Ed) thesis, University of Worcester.

Somekh, B. and Lewin, C. (2005) *Research Methods in Social Sciences*. London: Sage.

Spradley, J. P. (1979) *The Ethnographic Interview*. New York: Holt, Rinehart & Winston.

Stephenson, A. (2009) 'Horses in the sandpit: photography, prolonged involvement and "stepping back" as strategies for listening to children's voices', *Early Child Development and Care*, 179 (2): 131–41.

Stupnisky, R., Renaud, R., Daniels, L., Haynes, T. and Perry, R. (2007) 'The Interrelation of First-Year College Students' Critical Thinking Disposition, Perceived Academic Control, and Academic Achievement'. Online at: http://www.springerlink.com/content/33m6515205542167/fulltext.pdf.

Sylva, K., Mehuish, E., Simmons, P., Siraj-Blatchford, I. and Taggart, B. (2004) *Effective Provision of Pre-school Education Project: Final Report (EPPE)*. London: Institute of Education.

Tangen, R. (2008) 'Listening to children's voices in educational research: some theoretical and methodological problems', *European Journal of Special Needs Education*, 23 (2): 157–66.

Tight, M. (2010) 'The curious case of case study: a viewpoint', *International Journal of Social Research Methodology*, 13 (4): 329–39.

Tirado, F. and Galvez, B. (2007) 'Positioning theory and discourse analysis: some tools for social interaction analysis', *Forum: Qualitative Social Research*, 8 (2). Online at: http://www.qualitative-research.net/fqs/.

Tricoglus, G. (2001) 'Living the theoretical principals of critical ethnography', *Education Research*, 9 (1): 135–48.

Tyler, L. (2011 in press) '"Digiscape" extracted from: now we've got it, how do we know it's working? Evaluating the quality impact of technology in the early years', in M. Reed and N. Canning (eds), *Implementing Quality Improvement and Change in the Early Years*. London: Sage.

UNICEF (2007) 'Child Poverty in Perspective. An Overview: Child Well-being in Rich Counties'. Online at: http://www.unicef.org.

Wadsworth, Y. (1997) *Everyday Evaluation on the Run*, 2nd edn. Sydney: Allan & Unwin.

Webster-Wright, A. (2009) 'Reframing professional development through understanding authentic professional learning', *Review of Educational Research*, 79 (2): 702–39.

Wenger, E. (1998) *Communities of Practice: Learning, Meaning and Identity*. Cambridge: Cambridge University Press.

Wenger, E. (2010) 'Landscapes of Practice', a series of workshops held at the Practice-based Professional Learning Center for Excellence in Teaching and Learning, Open University, UK. Online at: http://www.open.ac.uk/blogs/LetsTalkPractice/ (publication in preparation available from the author).

Wenger, E., McDermott, R. and Snyder, W. (2002) *Cultivating Communities of Practice*. Boston: Harvard Business School Press.

Whitmarsh, J. (2007) 'Negotiating the moral maze: developing ethical literacy in multi-agency settings', in I. Siraj-Blatchford, K. Clarke and M. Needham (eds), *The Team Around the Child*. Stoke-on-Trent: Trentham Books.

Willis, P. (2004) 'Twenty five years on: old books, new times', in N. Dolby and G. Dimitriadis (eds), *Learning to Labour in New Times*. New York: Routledge.

Wohlwend, K. E. (2009) 'Mediated discourse analysis: researching young children's non-verbal interactions as a social practice', *Journal of Early Childhood Research*, 7: 228–43.

Yelland, N., Lee, L., O'Rourke, M. and Harrison, C. (2008) *Rethinking Learning in Early Education*. Maidenhead: Open University Press.

Index

The Body on the Island

Nick Louth is a best-selling thriller writer and an award-winning financial journalist. A 1979 graduate of the London School of Economics, he went on to become a Reuters foreign correspondent in 1987. He was for many years a *Financial Times* columnist, and a regular contributor to many other financial titles in print and online. *The Body on the Island* is his sixth book in the DCI Gillard crime series, and his ninth thriller overall. Nick Louth is married and lives in Lincolnshire.

www.nicklouth.com

Also by Nick Louth

Trapped
Heartbreaker

DCI Craig Gillard Crime Thrillers

The Body in the Marsh
The Body on the Shore
The Body in the Mist
The Body in the Snow
The Body Under the Bridge
The Body on the Island
The Bodies at Westgrave Hall
The Body on the Moor